A STUD
CHRISTIAN

D0194248

WHAT'CHA GONNA DO WITH WHAT'CHA GOT?

James W. Jackson

David C. Cook Publishing Co.
Elgin, Illinois—Weston, Ontario

What'cha Gonna Do with What'cha Got?
©1988 by James W. Jackson

93 92 91 90 89   5   4   3   2

All rights reserved. Except for brief excerpts for review purposes, no part of this book may be reproduced in any form without the written permission of the publisher.

Permission to quote from the following copyrighted versions of the Bible is acknowledged with appreciation: *The Living Bible* (TLB), ©1971 by Tyndale House Publishers, Wheaton, Illinois, and the *Holy Bible: New International Version,* ©1974 by the New York International Bible Society, New York, New York.

Published by David C. Cook Publishing Co.
850 N. Grove Ave., Elgin, IL 60120.
Cable Address: DCCOOK
Edited by Dave and Neta Jackson
Cover art: Bob Fuller
Design: Dawn Lauck
Printed in the United States of America
Library of Congress Catalog Number 87-72005
ISBN:1-55513-835-7

CONTENTS

■

SECTION ONE
What'cha Gonna Do with What'cha Got?

■ ■

SECTION TWO
Let's Discover What'cha Got

■ ■ ■
SECTION THREE
How'd You Get What'cha Got?

■ ■ ■ ■
SECTION FOUR
How to Use What'cha Got

F O R E W O R D

Perhaps there has never been a time in history when a book such as this has been needed by so many people. Financial pressures on today's families are very real. Churches and other charitable institutions are feeling the financial crunch. To a large degree, the pressure has resulted from the lack of good economic training available to people at the grass roots level.

James W. Jackson recognized the need . . . and decided to do something about it. He took the time to review his own experience and back it up with research. He is a successful businessman, author, and lecturer whose experience and education qualify him to present such a work. The book is not just economic theory, but it applies the principles to everyday life. His insight into and interpretation of today's economic situation reveals an understanding of money, the Federal Reserve system, and inflation. The subject matter is expressed so that the common person can comprehend. The investment strategy prescribed can be utilized by anyone. He explains the importance of frugality, and even takes you through the process of learning how to barter without the use of money.

The grasp on business and economic concepts is good, but the most important contribution is made by placing it all in the perspective of the Bible. The basic principles of God's economy, combines with classic economics results in CHRISTIANOMICS©.

The classic trilogy of *scarcity, choice,* and *cost* is applied to every part of life. The premise is that everything you possess is a scarce commodity, because it has alternative uses. It is up to you to decide what you will do with those commodities. The cost involved in those choices will greatly determine your life-style, both here and hereafter. So, as the book title asks . . .

"What'cha gonna do with what'cha got?"

1

Principles of God's Economy

I. A NEW AWAKENING

"We want to know more about God's economy, more about stewardship. We would like to learn these principles so that we can live with economic freedom and fulfillment. But no one will take the time to tell us how!"

Those words are still ringing in my ears. Ted and his lovely wife were attending a financial seminar I was conducting in a large western city. They approached me after a session, and I sensed that they were not there just to talk trivia. They were struggling with some major issues. Tears were in their eyes as they both expressed their deep desire, but no one had been able to help them.

Ted and his wife are representative of many people who are searching for the answers to economic freedom and fulfillment.

I believe that one of the most exciting phenomena taking place today is a rebirth of the desire to know more about God's basic economy. Calm minds that once rested in the security of a November election campaign promise are now troubled. In Detroit, the unemployed worker is beginning to reevaluate the validity of those incentive posters that used to hang on the cafeteria walls. In Pittsburgh, the president of a local savings and loan company is beginning to reassess his priorities. Maybe there is something in the economic scheme of things that has been overlooked.

God's prescribed principles certainly are not new, but, for the most part, they have been neglected. Today, those principles need to be rediscovered. In the chapters that follow, we are going to rediscover together some of those basic principles of God's economy.

Like many of you, I was exposed to many of those principles for most of my life, but I was not always wise enough to follow those principles. Other principles I have only recently come to understand.

My two brothers and I grew up together in a parsonage, which means, Pop was a preacher.

As kids we often heard Pop admonish the members of his small, struggling congregation to *follow the principles of God's economy.* And while we were still very young, he took us aside and explained to us, "Even though I can never give you much, I can show you how to get whatever you want." He not only took the time to instruct us in God's Word, but he also took the time to teach us the elementary concepts of business.

One day he brought home a New Zealand white rabbit, which soon had a scad of little fuzzy bunnies. He taught us the old barter system. He walked with us through the neighborhood and showed us how easy it was to trade those cute, fuzzy bunnies for almost anything. We were launched into business! Our vehicle: "Rabbit Transit!"

We walked behind our little red wagon, which was loaded with a couple of irresistible bunnies all nestled down in some freshly cut green grass. We would trade one of those bunnies for a marble collection or boy scout pocketknife. We would then take the marbles, the knife, and one more bunny, and trade them for a tricycle; take the trike and a matched pair of bunnies and trade for a bicycle, etc. By the time I was in junior high school, we were no longer trading rabbits; my brothers and I were trading for such things as cars.

During those years we were always encouraged to: "Take what you have and make it into what you want!"

I began to learn at an early age that *it is not so much what you have but what you do with it that makes all the difference in the world.* That concept is the great equalizing force of humanity. To the person who has very little of this world's talents or treasures, the question still comes: WHAT'CHA GONNA DO WITH WHAT'CHA GOT? To the person who seems to have a controlling grasp on Boardwalk, Park Place, and Pennsylvania Avenue, the question is still the same: WHAT'CHA GONNA DO WITH WHAT'CHA GOT? How you answer that question will determine the quality and character of your life here as well as hereafter.

Recall with me the episode that took place in the life of Moses when the Lord assured him:

"I know the King of Egypt isn't interested in letting you go . . .

except under heavy pressure. So I'll apply the pressure! If necessary, I'll destroy Egypt with My miracles. Then the King will beg you to go! In fact, Moses, when you leave the country, you will be loaded down with gifts: jewels, silver, gold, and you will clothe your sons and daughters with the best of Egypt!"

"Lord, this is too much!" responded Moses, "Nobody is going to believe me. I can't communicate this to my people. Remember, I have a terrible speech impediment!"

"Who makes mouths, Moses? Just do what I tell you, and I will help you."

"But, Lord, I don't have any resources."

"What do you have in your hand, Moses?"

"Just a shepherd's rod."

"Throw it down on the ground, Moses!"

"You mean my shepherd's rod?"

"Yes."

"But it's the only thing I have! I make my living with it!"

"Throw it down!"

"Well, all right, Lord, here goes. O Lord, let me out of here! My rod's become a hissing snake!"

"Pick up the snake, Moses . . . carefully now, by the tail."

"Look! It's become a rod again right here in my very own hands!"

"That's right, Moses. The only thing I ever wanted from you was what you have. Because, with that dedicated rod you will do some incredible but convincing miracles before Pharaoh. You will part the waters of the Red Sea. You will strike the rock and water will come gushing out. But you must be willing to let go of what you have."

In observing the life of Moses, I am reminded of an amazing fact: God, in His economy, never demands more from you than what you have. He will never ask you to give something that is out of your jurisdiction to give. Moses had a rod. *God only demanded the rod.* He didn't ask for Moses to surrender someone else's rod, only the one over which he had jurisdiction.

Even though God only requests of you things that are yours to give, you can count on the fact that He expects you to give back to Him at His request what you do have. That also seems extremely reasonable, since, like the old circuit-ridin' preacher used to say: "God can do a lot with a little if He has all there is of it." I believe that was the concept the apostle Paul was trying to explain to his friends in Corinth, when he said,

Having started the ball rolling so enthusiastically, you should carry this project through to completion just as gladly, giving whatever you can out of *whatever you have.* Let your enthusiastic idea at the start be equalled by your realistic action now. If you are really eager to give,

11

then it isn't important how much you have to give. *God wants you to give what you have, not what you haven't* (II Cor. 8:11, 12, TLB emphasis added).

Don't fret over what you do not have to give, or what you wish you had to give, or what someone else has to give. God is not concerned about that. What He is concerned about is, *What are you doing with what you have?* And, of course, that is the only realm where you can make valid choices.

Answering the question, "WHAT'CHA GONNA DO WITH WHAT'CHA GOT?" is an important key to learning more about God's economy, knowing more about stewardship, and discovering more about the basic principles that will help you live with economic freedom and fulfillment.

II. SIX PRINCIPLES OF GOD'S ECONOMY

God is eager to help you understand the principles as you make yourself *available*.

A. Principle 1: God Has Given

Everything that you have and enjoy has been given by God. He requires nothing from you that He has not already given to you. The psalmist portrays God as the absolute and ultimate Source.

> O Lord, what a variety you have made! And in wisdom *you have made them all!* The earth is full of your riches.
> There before me lies the mighty ocean, teeming with life of every kind, both great and small. And look! See the ships! And over there, the whale you made to play in the sea. Every one of these depends on you to give them daily food. *You supply it,* and they gather it. You open wide your hand to feed them and they are satisfied with all your *bountiful provision* (Ps. 104:24-28, TLB, emphasis added).

When I was teaching a small-group Bible study, a sharp young attorney posed an interesting question to me. "In God's economy," he asked, "does He expect us to give first?" After discussing the proposition for a while, we concluded that it would be impossible. God already holds that distinctive position. He has already given first. I directed the young attorney's attention to an interesting Scripture. King David was turning the throne over to his son Solomon, having gathered together all the riches necessary to build the Temple. David prayed this prayer:

> Everything in the heavens and earth is yours, O Lord, and this is your kingdom. We adore you as being in control of everything. . . .

Everything we have has come from you, and we only give you what is yours already! For we are here for but a moment, strangers in the land as our fathers were before us; our days on earth are like a shadow, gone so soon, without a trace. O Lord our God, all of this material that we have gathered to build a temple for your holy name *comes from you! It all belongs to you!* (I Chr. 29:11-16 TLB, emphasis added).

King David realized that without God's great benevolent act of giving first, we would never have the opportunity to give at all! God's entire economic system is based on the fact that He has already given.

B. Principle 2: God Is Looking for a People

God has always had a people who were convinced enough of His integrity that they would risk their lives and possessions on His economic principles. He wants to locate those people today who will make themselves available to allow the plan to work through them. "For the eyes of the Lord search back and forth across the whole earth, looking for people whose hearts are perfect toward him, *so that* he can show his great power in helping them" (II Chr. 16:9, TLB, emphasis added).

The Bible is a record of the fact that when God can find a handful of people who will allow His principles to work through them, the course of history can be altered. One of those committed persons was the prophet Haggai. He courageously called the people of his day to examine the economic principles by which they were living.

You plant much but harvest little. You have scarcely enough to eat or drink, and not enough clothes to keep you warm. *Your income disappears, as though you were putting it into pockets filled with holes!*

You hope for much but get so little. And when you bring it home, I blow it away—it doesn't last at all. Why? Because my Temple lies in ruins *and you don't care.* Your only concern is your own fine homes. That is why I am holding back the rains from heaven and giving you such scant crops (Hag. 1:6, 9, 10, TLB, emphasis added).

Haggai was calling on them to face the age-old question: "WHAT'CHA GONNA DO WITH WHAT'CHA GOT?"

An exciting thing happened! A handful of people responded positively to Haggai's challenge, and they began to allow God's principles to work in their lives.

Then Zerubbabel (son of She-alti-el), the governor of Judah, and Joshua (son of Josedech), the High Priest, and the *few people* remaining in the land obeyed Haggai's message from the Lord their God; they began or worship him in earnest (Hag. 1:12, TLB, emphasis added).

All it took was a few . . . just a handful of people to change the events of history. The Lord told them,

> Take courage and work, for "I am with you" . . . "The future splendor of this Temple will be greater than the splendor of the first one! *For I have plenty of silver and gold to do it!* And here I will give peace," says the Lord (Hag. 2:4, 9, TLB, emphasis added).

God was eager to bless the handful of obedient people. He even promised to begin blessing them from the time they decided to allow the principles to begin working through them.

> But now note this: From today, this 24th day of the month, as the foundation of the Lord's Temple is finished, and from this day onward, I will bless you. Notice, I am giving you this promise now before you have even begun, to rebuild the Temple structure, and before you have harvested your grain, and before the grapes and figs and pomegranates and olives have produced their next crops: "From this day I will bless you" (Hag. 2:16-19, TLB).

The principles in Haggai are consistently transferable to those who would be *quickly and completely obedient* today.

The dedicated life of Dwight L. Moody has always intrigued me. When the searching eyes of the Lord found Moody, they found a man whose *availability* far outdistanced his *ability*. But God can do a lot with a little if He has all there is of it!

Moody was born in 1837 in the little town of Northfield, Mass. His father died at 41, leaving his widow in poverty with a large mortgage on the home. The creditors grabbed everything they could, including the firewood. It's said that the family was so poor that the boys would carry their shoes and stockings to church to keep them from wearing out and put them on only when they were in sight of the church.

By the time Dwight was 17, he had become a successful show salesman for Holton's Show Store. Moody accepted Christ in the back room of the shoe store through the guidance of his Sunday School teacher. Later, he became actively involved in the Plymouth Congregational Church of Chicago. As a layman, he began renting the church pews and filling them up with men and women whom he had invited.

By the time Moody was 30, he decided to sell his business and devote all of his time to Christian work. He traveled to Dublin, Ireland, where on a bench in a public park, Mr. Henry Varley shared with him: "The world has yet to see what God will do with and for and through and in and by the man who is fully consecrated to Him."

That conversation absolutely changed Dwight L. Moody's life. As he reflected on Varley's words, the simple but profound light broke in upon his mind: "He said *a man*. He did not say, a great man, nor a learned man, not a *smart* man, but simply *a man*. I am a man, and it lies within the man himself whether he will or will not make that entire and full consecration. I will try my utmost to be that man."

Moody went from there to become one of the greatest influences for right of all time. It is estimated that no less that 100 *million* people heard the Gospel from the lips of Dwight L. Moody.

C. Principle 3: God's Economy Is Not Based on Greed

The spirit of greed is in direct opposition to the spirit set forth in God's economy. However, even though it is in direct opposition, greed is not always clearly identifiable to the observer. Sometimes you can see it, sometimes you cannot.

Instruction is clearly given in the Scriptures that God's economy is not based on greed. "The kingdom of Christ and of God will never belong to anyone who is impure or greedy, for a greedy person is really an idol worshiper—he loves and worships the good things of this life more than God" (Eph. 5:5, TLB). Christ even scolded the people who were hanging around just for what they could receive: "The truth of the matter is that you want to be with me because I fed you, not because you believe in me" (Jn. 6:26, TLB).

The Bible is full of examples of folks who discovered that, *in the end, greed delivers a different result than they had anticipated in the beginning*: Eve—in desiring the forbidden fruit (Gen. 3:6), Lot—in choosing the lush valley (Gen. 13:10), Jacob—in defrauding Esau (Gen. 27:6), Saul—in sparing King Agag and the livestock (I Sam. 15:8), David and Bathsheba—in cheating on Uriah (II Sam. 11:2), Achan—in stealing the booty (Josh. 7:21), and Gehazi—in taking the gifts from Naaman (II Ki. 5:20).

One of the tragic examples of trying to merge greed into God's economy is that of Simon Magus (Acts 8:18). Simon lived in Samaria where Philip was having tremendous success in his evangelistic work. Simon, who was a popularity seeker, was attracted to Philip's success. He wanted a part of the action. When Peter and John arrived on the scene to help establish Philip's ministry, Simon observed their power to impart miraculous things by the laying of hands. People were awed; the excitement was high. Simon has awed the Samaritans before with cheap trickery, but this was much bigger. So he went to Peter and John and offered to buy the power of conferring spiritual gifts. Well, he found out that God's economy was not based on greed. Peter rebuked him in such stern language that it prompted Simon to beg for mercy to escape the severe judgment of God.

Sometimes God's judgment in dealing with greed is not immediate, and He allows greed to run its natural course, and the sad results are only visible later.

God's economy is not based on greed, because greed is inconsistent with God's nature: "Purity is best demonstrated by generosity" (Lk. 11:41, TLB). God, who has already generously given, is looking for a people who will be characterized by *giving*, not *grabbing*.

D. Principle 4: God Always Repays When You Give . . . but You Don't Give to Get

Although this principle relates in some ways to the previous principle, it is distinct enough to merit its own category.

An interesting phenomenon has developed. It is subtle. It has immediate appeal. Like a counterfeit bill, the distinction between it and authenticity is sometimes difficult to detect. It implies that, since God's principles are *predictable*, they are *manipulatable*.

I was listening to a radio evangelist who was in financial trouble. He was pleading with the people that, if they would send him $100, God would guarantee to give them at least $1000 by the end of the year. I pricked up my ears. I was curious as to whether God had filed a prospectus with the Securities Exchange Commission.

I thought about that episode for a long time. So many things about it were right . . . but so many things about it were wrong! A short time later I was counseling with a disillusioned, discouraged couple who had responded to a similar appeal. They had given their money; the guarantee time had expired; and they had received nothing back. They were very hostile toward God. They claimed that they had done their part, and God had "goofed" . . . and the only guarantee left was the guarantee that they would never be made fools of again.

I was reminded of that verse in Romans: "And who could ever offer to the Lord enough to induce him to act?" (Rom. 11:35, TLB). The problem with dealing with a half-truth is that you are likely to get hold of the wrong half.

It is certain that God always repays when you give. That is part of His economy. But the selfish motive of "giving to get" is not part of the deal. Oswald Chambers, in *My Utmost for His Highest* (New York: Dodd, Mead, & Co., 1965, p. 72), states,

Our Lord replies in effect, that abandonment is for Himself, and not for what the disciples themselves will get from it. Beware of an abandonment which has the commercial spirit in it . . . If we only give up something to God because we want more back, there is nothing of the Holy Spirit in our abandonment; it is miserable commercial self-interest.

16

In this book there will be found no schemes to scare God into a corner, no "10 Easy Lessons on How to Bring God to the Bargaining Table." However, you will find the good news that you can enter into a relationship with God where you give to Him, and you don't care if He ever gives it back to you *in this life*. It is a relationship that the prophet Habakkuk was explaining to the people of his day:

> Even though the fig trees are all destroyed, and there is neither blossom left nor fruit, and though the olive crops all fail, and the fields lie barren; even if the flocks die in the fields and the cattle barns are empty, yet I will rejoice in the Lord; I will be happy in the God of my salvation (Hab. 3:17, 18, TLB).

E. Principle 5: God's Multiplication Begins with Your Subtraction

One of the principles taught throughout the Bible declares that as you *subtract* your rights of ownership to what you possess, God has the opportunity to *bless and multiply* it for *His purposes*.

Christ consistently taught the concept in His daily ministry: "For whosoever will save his life shall lose it: and whosoever will lose his life for my sake shall find it" (Mt. 16:25, KJV). This sounds strange when you first hear it. But Solomon found the principle to be valid, and exclaimed, "It is possible to give away and become richer! It is also possible to hold on too tightly and lose everything. Yes, the liberal man shall be rich! By watering others, he waters himself" (Prov. 11:24, 25, TLB). He was not just talking in riddles, he was trying to communicate an extremely important principle. The things that you hold onto so tightly in life are the things that usually have a way of being squeezed out through your fingers. The tighter you squeeze . . . the more they slip away. But the things that you are willing to release are the things that multiply.

I often think of Johnny Appleseed walking through the countryside of the New Frontier. He knew that if the countryside was to be covered with apple trees, he would have to take those seeds out of his grubby pocket, let go of them, bury them in the ground, and walk away. He couldn't even come back 90 days later, dig them up, and see how they were doing. But, as he released his rights to them, the miracle took place.

Picture yourself eavesdropping as Andrew approached the lad with the five loaves and two fish on the Galilean hillside.

"What'cha got in your knapsack, Son?"

"Guess."

"Well, I'd say fish!"

"How'd ya know?"

"I used to be a professional fisherman. I've got a nose for 'em! Tell me something; what'cha gonna do with what'cha got?"

Just suppose the little kid would have told Andrew: "Go mind your own business and quit trying to take food away from someone smaller than you."

I wonder how that story would have ended? But I'm *glad* the little fellow learned that "Your care for others is the measure of your greatness" (Lk. 9:48, TLB). I am also glad that he was able to discover that, *as he released his possessions*, God was then able to bless and *multiply* them to the benefit of *His Kingdom*. If you are obedient to God and faithful with what He has entrusted to you . . . then He enjoys multiplying what He already owns for the sake of advancing His Kingdom business.

Recall with me the interesting episode that occurred in the life of that rough, old mountain man of God, Elijah. There was drought and famine in the land when the Lord told him:

> "Go and live in the village of Zarephath, near the city of Sidon. There is a widow there who will feed you. I have given her my instructions."
>
> So he went to Zarephath. As he arrived at the gates of the city he saw a widow gathering sticks; and he asked her for a cup of water.
>
> As she was going to get it, he called to her, "Bring me a bite of bread, too."
>
> But she said, "I swear by the Lord your God that I haven't a single piece of bread in the house. And I have only a handful of flour left and a little cooking oil in the bottom of the jar. I was just gathering a few sticks to cook this last meal, and then my son and I must die of starvation."
>
> But Elijah said to her, "Don't be afraid! Go ahead and cook that 'last meal,' but bake me a little loaf of bread first; and afterwards there will still be enough food for you and your son. For the Lord God of Israel says that there will always be plenty of flour and oil left in your containers until the time when the Lord sends rain, and the crops grow again!" (I Ki. 17:8b-14, TLB).

Little did the lady know that hundreds of years forward in the pageant of time, the Messiah Himself would say:

> All mankind scratches for its daily bread, but your heavenly Father knows your needs. He will always give you all you need from day to day if your will *make the Kingdom of God your primary concern* (Lk. 12:30, 31, TLB, emphasis added).

Or little did she know that Elijah's great-great-great cousin, the apostle Paul, would write: "My God shall supply all your need according to his riches in glory by Christ Jesus" (Phil. 4:19, KJV).

18

Well, did the widow woman starve to death? What happened to Elijah?

> So *she did as Elijah said,* and she and Elijah and her son continued to eat from her supply of flour and oil as long as it was needed. *For no matter how much they used, there was always plenty left* in the containers, just as the Lord had promised through Elihah! (I Ki. 17:15, 16, TLB).

The widow woman discovered an interesting aspect of God's economy. Her inventory was limited. If she had relied on her supply alone, she and her son would have certainly died of starvation. However, through surrender, she tapped into a never-failing sufficiency. God's supply knows no shortage.

F. Principle 6: God's Economic Success Will Cost You Everything You Value More Than Him

In God's economy you are always admonished to sit down and count the cost. There is a cost that must be considered when dealing with God's principles. When some folks become aware of the cost they back away. However, there are others who simply need someone to help them turn over the tag so they can understand the price.

Every situation of your life includes alternatives. Alternatives demand choices. You must continually choose the alternative you most highly desire. The cost of the alternative you choose is the value of the next highest alternative that was foregone in selecting it. In other words, the cost is the value of the alternative you might have had but decided to do without.

For example, the cost of the alternative chosen by the prodigal son—to run away to a foreign country—was foregoing the value of staying home where he had security, good food, and acceptance.

The apostle Paul realized that the cost of the choice to serve Jesus was the foregoing of the value of the alternative of becoming a well-known leader of the Pharisees, with men under his command, and power at his disposal. In God's economy, success will cost you the foregoing of those alternatives that are not consistent with His principles.

In my own personal life, I recall the adventure of working through the cost concept as it applied to the question of "What'cha gonna do with what'cha got?" Having grown up in a minister's home and having given my life to Christ, I assumed that I would become a preacher. It was my senior year in high school when it really hit me for the first time that maybe the Lord didn't want me to be a preacher. Maybe He wanted me to do something else!

That possibility came as a shock! "Lord, You must have this whole thing wrong," I said. "Don't You remember? I'm committed to You, and committed means I either have to be a missionary like my Uncle Bob and Aunt Lela in Africa, or like my Uncle Chester in Japan, or a preacher like Pop. And I'd rather be a preacher like Pop."

Isn't it strange, but in all my growing-up years, nobody told me that it was *possible to be called to be a totally dedicated businessman!*

However, quite sure that God was mistaken, I entered college with a Religion/Philosophy major. I soon married my junior high and high school sweetheart, who went through the process of committing herself to becoming a loyal, devoted preacher's wife!

But just in case, I pushed myself to graduate with a double major: religion/philosophy and secondary education. Then, the next year while Anne finished her degree, I commuted to a neighboring college where I received a master's degree. Little did I know what was happening! I was *rapidly* accumulating an inventory of possessions that I would ultimately be responsible for when faced with that historic question: "What'cha gonna do with what'cha got?"

Then at the general assembly convention of our church denomination, a pastor from a large church in Denver invited me to come and be his minister of music. "The folks who presently hold the position are going to head back to Des Moines," he said, "and we would love to have you just as soon as you could come."

So we sold our little businesses, loaded up everything we could, and headed for Denver. But when we arrived, the pastor said, "Uh . . . sit down. Nice to have you here. Uh, we have a little problem. . . . The folks who are the ministers of music have decided *not* to go back to Des Moines—nothing major . . . I'm sure! You see, another wonderful couple who serve as our ministers of youth and education, will soon be leaving to go to Montana and if you don't mind switching hats, we will just move you right into that spot. You're qualified to do either."

I looked around the room, out the open door onto the patio area— 900 miles away from home—and realized I wasn't in much of a bargaining position. So, I said, "Okay. Fine."

But about six weeks later the pastor said, "The wonderful couple who are serving as our ministers of youth and education have decided not to move back to Montana until their kids graduate from Englewood High School. Sorry."

Again, I said, "Okay. Fine." But it wasn't fine at all. Why had we felt so strongly that we should move to Denver? Why had God brought us 900 miles from home and dumped us? It was even too late to get a teaching job! As the Colorado winter sky began to get dark and gray and heavy, so did I, inside. For the first time in my life, I began to question the integrity of God. I discovered something: As I began to question God's integrity . . . none of the old promises seemed to make sense anymore. In fact, I seemed to eliminate some of the frustration by simply not reading the Word anymore.

I began doing the only thing I knew to do: I began trading—not rabbits but cars.

Sometime later we had moved from the church. By then we had two boys, and I was in business in Denver with my two brothers. We were loving it! But what about church? Strange, it didn't seem so all-important anymore. I wanted Annie and Doug and Jay in church, but, as for me, I really didn't miss it.

Something else was strange. As we were meeting defeat in our hearts, we were meeting success in our finances. That's not the way they said it would work. I had dreams of becoming a millionaire by age 25. Then it hit! All those beautiful sand castles came down. Suddenly we were $204,000 in the hole. An attorney told us, "It appears that you have two choices: bankruptcy or suicide."

We weren't ready for either. One night over a ten-cent cup of coffee in the Greek Village Restaurant on South Santa Fe, three brothers pledged that even if it took working 20-hour days the rest of our lives, we were going to pay it all back, learn from our mistakes, and then build from there.

From out of somewhere in the past, we remembered the Scripture:

> Two can accomplish more than twice as much as one, for the results can be much better. If one falls, the other pulls him up; but if a man falls when he is alone, he's in trouble. And one standing alone can be attacked and defeated, but two can stand back-to-back and conquer; three is even better, for a triple-braided cord is not easily broken (Eccl. 4:9, 10, 12, TLB).

A brilliant idea hit us: *Why don't we try using the trading techniques and barter system on real estate!*

The middle and late 1960s was the perfect time to get into real estate in Colorado, especially in the ski areas. And the marketplace was ready for trading and bartering. During the "good times" we had purchased 10 acres right in the heart of one of the ski towns. We began to develop it. Before long we were in partnership with the lieutenant governor of Colorado on another project. Within 18 months we had satisfied all the old debts with never a "slow" on our credit. It was taking the 20 hours a day, but it was paying off. Soon that new financial statement was far surpassing any previous statement—by a long shot!

Our church got a new pastor, and it wasn't very long until he began looking up the Jackson brothers. He invited us to lunch, then to breakfast; he seemed to know when we were in town. He began telling us about some of his dreams for the church that was at that time running about 225-250 in attendance. He started asking us questions about our business. My interest was aroused.

We were working at one of our projects in the mountains. It was in a little town at the base of the famed Winter Park ski slopes called Hideaway Park. We were building a post office on one corner of the property to insure good traffic flow for the rest of the property. I recall talking to my brother, Bill, about the church situation in general.

"Do you suppose," I asked, "that all those dreams we had when we were little kids about a church really doing something significant are dead? Or do you think that there might still be a chance?" Bill just shrugged his shoulders and went back to work. But I knew what was happening deep inside of me. The faithfulness of the Holy Spirit was gently bringing me to a point of decision.

That evening as we made our way back to our condominium, I was unusually quiet. The condominium was located on another one of our projects that sat on a high bluff overlooking the beautiful Frazier Valley. Sometimes you could stand on the balcony of the condominium and watch the silver and red fox working their way through the brush along the Frazier River in search of their dinner. After we had eaten and talked about the next day's work, we all headed for our bedrooms. But as the wind howled around the building that night and through the lodge-pole pine trees, I found my way back out to the living room. There with the sparking embers still glowing in the little fireplace, I knelt beside the sofa and wept my back to God. "Forgive me for all those wasted years," I prayed. "Forgive me for my rotten attitudes. I want more than anything else to be Yours and fit into Your plans."

Next day I got into the car and headed back to Denver to find our new pastor and tell him what had happened. In the months that followed, we began to share some of our old dreams, and he began to share more of his. We decided to see if we could put some financial arms and legs to those dreams. The business, Jackson Brothers Investments, Ltd., was continually growing like crazy: income properties, developments, our own luxury homes in the mountains. At one time we Jacksons had ten Mercedes Benz between the three of us. But, with my brothers' encouragement, I began getting terribly involved in the church.

One of my involvements was singing in a musical group with two other guys. We were getting ready for a recording session, and we were rehearsing late at the church. It was about one o'clock in the morning when I headed for home. I was driving a Mercedes 600 Grand Limousine. Probably you have never seen one unless it was on TV: beautiful midnight blue with all gray leather interior, curtains all the way around the back windows, air-conditioning coils under the floor mats (to keep your feet cool on hot days) and even a hydraulically reclining backseat. The doors only had to close part way, and then they would close and latch automatically. Truly Mercedes Benz's pride and joy! I liked it, too. But I'll never forget that night . . . March 12.

We live in a little town just 35 miles west of Denver called Evergreen. It's a little European-type town nestled around a lake, between the front range and the back range of the great Rocky Mountains. As I headed up Highway 285, it was one of the most beautiful nights I had ever seen. The bright moon on the fresh Colorado powder snow made the stately blue spruce trees sparkle as though they were trimmed with diamonds. I reached over and turned off the radio.

"God," I said, "I just want to talk to You. Thank You for making everything so beautiful. Thank You for changing my life and for what's happening with Annie and Doug and Jay."

As I was praying, God's presence seemed to fill that car until I felt that if I looked, He would be sitting there in that plush gray leather seat next to me. "Jim, do you really love Me?" He asked in a voice that was more real to the senses than if it had been audible.

"Of course I do, Lord. Don't You remember where I've been all night . . . doing Your thing? Of course I love You."

"Jim, would you love Me like you do tonight if I took *everything* that you have accumulated *away from you?*"

By that time the warm tears were freely coursing down my face as I tried to keep that big car on the road. As I thought about the question, the inventory from the financial statement began to click through my mind: offices, warehouses, apartments, properties in Denver, Colorado Springs, Manitou Springs, etc. . . . Suddenly the answer snapped into focus in my mind: "Sure, God, I'd love You the same, even if You took it all away . . . because remember we started out with less than nothing, and now I know the formulas and the people, and I could get it all back again. Sure."

That wasn't exactly what He wanted to hear. It was real quiet for a while. Then: "Son, what if I even took your abilities to accumulate for yourself, would you love Me the same as you do tonight?"

I was crushed that I hadn't seen what He was getting at before. I wept with no reserve. There in that beautiful but awesome setting, I had been faced with that same simple, but inescapable, historic question: "What'cha gonna do with what'cha got?"

I prayed a lot more as I drove those last few miles on home. I parked the car in the garage and stood for a long time overlooking the frozen lake. "God, if You really want to do business, I'm ready to do business with You." I made my way up the stairs and into the beautiful, large living room of my house. I sat down, took out a pen and piece of paper. "Please, God, be faithful to me. If there is anything that would alter or hinder or block the flow of Your life or Your ministry through me, please show it to me, and I will write it down and take care of it . . . anything You want me to do."

When I finished, it was about three o'clock in the morning. I was physically and emotionally drained, but I slept well! The next morning I got up and there on the dresser was that same crazy piece of paper, with the 11 things that I had written on it a few hours before. In a flash I recalled the entire evening.

I really don't understand some of the 11 things on that paper yet. I'm anxious to get to Heaven and find out what some of them were all about. For example, one of them was to sit down and write a letter to a good Catholic doctor with whom we had done some real estate business, and simply tell him what Christ had done in my life and the lives of my family. Result? *Nothing* that I know of! One of the things that did make sense, however, was the instruction to go down and buy my sophisticated brother Dave one of those hard-backed, green *Living Bibles*. It wasn't long until Dave started showing up at our Tuesday morning Bible study with the new Bible and everything! Today he, his lovely wife Patty, and their four beautiful daughters are all a very integral part of the church fellowship.

Without doubt, the toughest requirement on the list had to do with my oldest brother, Bill. But I can take you to the little restaurant on Littleton Blvd., to a small table in the far corner of that restaurant where the two of us went for dinner that night. I guess it was sort of the ultimate thing I had to face in seeing if I was really serious about following through on that question: "What'cha gonna do with what'cha got?"

In any case, that night I signed over all my interests in our business, the office buildings, apartments, mobile home parks, subdivisions—everything. I told him I just wanted to start over. And, "if God ever allows me to put together another business deal, I want it to be for Kingdom business."

Even though Bill wasn't right with God at the time, I had always known him to be kind and fair and extremely tenderhearted. He had recently been through a very agonizing, traumatic divorce, and that night as we left the restaurant, I noticed that his shoulders were sagging under the added shock of the evening. My feelings were mixed. I was torn up, too! I felt grief, but I felt a release! I felt like a rotten bum, but I felt victoriously obedient!

The next morning Bill came in and began to share with me something that was more exciting than all the deals in the world. He described how he had gone home the night before to his big, beautiful home on Upper Bear Creek in Evergreen (where he lived by himself), got down on his knees beside an old antique rocking chair in front of the fireplace in his master bedroom, and with deep contrition, wept his way back into the family of God. "Jimmy," he said, "I really don't want any of that stuff personally either. Let's see how fast we can transfer those assets out of the hands of the prince of this world into Kingdom business."

And that's what we set about to do. *What a reunion!* Those were exciting days.

Years later a man said to me, "I've heard about you, and I want you to know that if God blessed me like He blessed you, *it wouldn't be hard for me to give all that money either.* . . ." I could only smile at him and tell him that for his comment I had no rebuttal. What could I say? I realized that he had not the foggiest idea of the price that had been paid to accumulate those assets.

As he was talking, I had an interesting series of instant replay flashbacks: One was when we were trying desperately to fight our way back from financial chaos. I could see my little boy sitting in a high chair in a dinky duplex on Crestline Avenue. He was asking his mom and dad why he had to eat carrots for breakfast . . . "Cause it's all we've got, and besides, they are good for your eyesight . . . I never did have one of my little rabbits that had to wear glasses!"

Another was when I pulled down a box of cornmeal—the last thing we had in the house to eat. But we discovered it to be full of weevils! We carefully picked out the weevils . . . and ate the cornmeal!

I encouraged the young man to not even attempt to imagine how difficult or how easy it would be to surrender something that did not belong to him. But rather, I encouraged him to be sensitive as he reviewed his own personal inventory and answered that great equalizing question: "What'cha gonna do with what'cha got?"

Your choices will always cost you everything you value more than Jesus.

2

Your Personal Possession Portfolio

Success in a business is closely tied to *inventory control*. It's difficult to merchandise a product that you don't realize is in your warehouse. When God gives you a blessing or a possession, He expects you to keep track of it. He wants you to realize *what* it is, *where* it is, and *how* it came into your possession. Being aware of your inventory produces a basis for gratitude:

> *Count your blessings,*
> *Name them one by one,*
> *Count your many blessings,*
> *See what God has done.*
> —Johnson Oatman, Jr.

Inventory awareness also allows you to function as a more responsible *steward.* God has always been in favor of your keeping good inventory records—so that He can have ready access to what He has entrusted to you.

Chapter One provided an overview of the basic principles of God's economy. But now it's time to discover some *practical handles* for your personal possession portfolio.

In a spiral notebook or a loose-leaf binder, create work sheets of a usable size for each of those summarized on the pages to follow. On them you will be asked to list *everything* you possess. You will not be able to accomplish such an assignment in ten minutes, so keep your notebook and your pen handy for the next couple of days. Ask the aid of the Holy Spirit to bring things to your mind. No doubt, your natural tendency will be to underestimate yourself and your possessions, thereby understanding the inheritance God has given to you. But remember what Paul said: "As God's messenger I give each of you God's warning: *Be honest in your estimate of yourselves . . .*" (Rom. 12:3, TLB, emphasis added).

I. FINANCIAL POSSESSIONS

First let's discover the value of your financial possessions through the "equity" approach. In order to find the equity of each item, take the *current replacement value* (what it would cost you to go out and replace it in today's market) of the possession and *subtract any indebtedness.*

EXAMPLE: YOUR HOME

Current replacement value	$100,000
Indebtedness	60,000
Equity	$ 40,000

	AMOUNT
Cash on hand or in banks	_____
Savings accounts or credit union accounts	_____
Cash value in retirement benefits	_____
Tax returns due me	_____
Loans due me	_____
Accounts due me	_____
Stocks owned	_____
Bonds owned	_____
Value in profit sharing or pension plan	_____
Equity in my business	_____
Equity in partnerships	_____
Equity in my home	_____
Equity in other city property	_____
Equity in country real estate	_____
Equity in cabin or second home	_____
Life insurance (cash value only)	_____

Auto: (owned not leased)

year: _____ make: _____ equity: _____

year: _____ make: _____ equity: _____

year: _____ make: _____ equity: _____

Equity in household goods:
  Furniture _____
  Appliances _____
  Drapes and carpet _____
  Kitchenware _____
  Bedding and bath linen _____
  Food supplies _____
  Medical supplies _____
Equity in personal property:
  Wardrobe _____
  Home shop equipment _____
  Yard and lawn equipment _____
  Recreational equipment: _____

  _____ _____

  _____ _____
  Jewelry, gems, rings _____
  Antiques _____
  Personal property located in other real estate _____
  Related business inventories (e.g., Amway,
    Shaklee, etc.) _____
Other Financial Assets:

  _____ _____

  _____ _____

  _____ _____

  _____ _____

TOTAL EQUITY $ _____

By taking the "equity" approach, you have accounted for all debts owed against your listed financial possessions.

Now, list any additional debts that you have which you have not already subtracted from the above debt.

ADDITIONAL DEBTS: AMOUNT
  Credit card accounts _____
  Educational loans _____
  Personal loans _____
  Judgments _____
  Back alimony or child support _____

_____   _____
_____   _____

TOTAL $ _____

TOTAL OF EQUITIES LISTED ABOVE $ _____
LESS ADDITIONAL DEBTS $ _____
TOTAL NET EQUITY $ _____

II. PERSONAL POSSESSIONS

Evaluating your personal possessions becomes a little more complex than simply making a list and attaching a dollar sign to its marketplace value. Certainly these personal evaluations will be more subjective.

A. Physical Possessions

1. List five to eight physical characteristics that you like about *yourself.*
2. List five to eight physical characteristics that *others have said they like about you.*
3. List the physical characteristics that *you intend to improve upon or totally change.*
4. List the physical characteristics which you cannot change, which *you need to accept by a change of attitude.*

B. Intellectual Possessions

1. List the intellectual areas where you have strength. Below are a few possible suggestions.

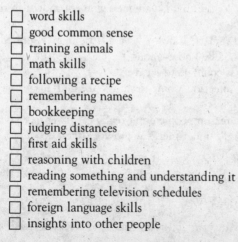

- ☐ word skills
- ☐ good common sense
- ☐ training animals
- ☐ math skills
- ☐ following a recipe
- ☐ remembering names
- ☐ bookkeeping
- ☐ judging distances
- ☐ first aid skills
- ☐ reasoning with children
- ☐ reading something and understanding it
- ☐ remembering television schedules
- ☐ foreign language skills
- ☐ insights into other people

☐ puns or humor with words
☐ filling out my own income tax return
☐ figuring out compass directions
☐ figuring out how to repair a kitchen appliance
☐ remembering telephone numbers

2. List the number of years of formal education that you have completed, and name the subjects of education that you enjoy most.
3. As you recall your years of formal education, list the subjects which you disliked most.
4. Using three adjectives, generally describe your intellectual abilities.
5. List three to five areas of interest that you have and would like to better understand or pursue if you had the opportunity.

C. Emotional Possessions

You will be able to discover some of your unique emotional characteristics if you will discuss the following statements in a group setting. But, first, go through the list and put a plus (+) or minus (-) by each statement according to whether you agree or disagree. Then be ready to defend your position in a group discussion.

1. I think it's silly to be afraid of the dark.
2. I think that there is nothing as beautiful as a sunrise.
3. There is nothing as irritating as a crying kid.
4. People who go to a ball game and yell a lot are weird.
5. I think men who cry are weak.
6. The only people who have chills when they hear "The Star-Spangled Banner" or see the flag are men who got shot at in the war.
7. Because I think it's smart, I always keep a little money stashed away where no one else knows about it.
8. I sure wish animals could go to Heaven.
9. Letting your true affections show toward someone is a sure way of getting hurt.
10. I believe that the reason people don't really get upset more often is because they don't understand the problem like I do.

In your notebook list the three words that would best describe your emotional characteristics.

D. Volitional Possessions

Your *volition* is your will, your ability to choose. This section will deal with your decision-making characteristics. Beside the following decision-making characteristics place an "M" next to those that describe you, an "F" by those that indicate how your friends see you, and an "I" beside your ideals.

1. I come off at first like I'm really stubborn, but that's only to buy time enough to figure out what's happening.
2. If we are going out to eat, the family always looks to me to make the decision as to *where*.
3. I wish someone else would pick out the clothes that I'm going to wear to church.
4. "It's alright, whatever you decide, as long as it's my suggestion that you choose."
5. I get physically upset whenever I'm faced with a major decision.
6. I have found out that if I can stall and "buy enough time," I don't have to make many decisions.
7. When the kids want a decision, they always come to me.
8. As a decision maker, I have a reputation to live up to.
9. "It's almost unbelievable that you don't like my idea."
10. "If I'm convinced of something, you may as well forget it. I'm not going to change my mind."
11. Sometimes I worry about not having all the facts when I'm forced to make a decision.
12. People *honk* a lot at me in traffic.
13. I would just as soon let someone else make *all* the decisions.
14. I like to be the first one to order in a restaurant.
15. I believe that a group is wiser than an individual.

In summary, list what would best describe your decision-making characteristics.

E. Temporal Possessions

Time is the measure of duration. *Today* is one of your possessions. It is the one commodity that you trade for everything else. Take a moment to figure out how many days you have been alive. Multiply your age by 365.25 days; then add the number of days since your last birthday.

Based on the Biblical idea of "threescore years and ten" (70 years; Ps. 90:10, KJV), how many days could one generally expect to live? Now subtract the number of days you have already lived to get an ideal of the theoretical number left. Actuarial tables show that the older one is, the greater the likelihood of going beyond the 70 years.

31

III. RELATIONAL POSSESSIONS

A. Family

In your notebook fill out a page with the following information.

Your name _____ Age _____

Spouse's name (if married) _____ Age _____

Your parents' names: (if living)	Father _____	Age _____
	Mother _____	Age _____
Your grandparents' names: (if living)	Grandfather _____	Age _____
	Grandmother _____	Age _____
Spouse's parents' names: (if living)	Father _____	Age _____
	Mother _____	Age _____
Spouse's grandparents' names: (if living)	Grandfather _____	Age _____
	Grandfather _____	Age _____

Children (if any): (write out full name— include all children even if they are not living with you)	Name _____	Age _____
	Name _____	Age _____
	Name _____	Age _____
	Name _____	Age _____
	Name _____	Age _____
	Name _____	Age _____

Brothers and sisters: (if living)	Name _____
	Name _____
	Name _____
	Name _____

Brothers-in-law and sisters-in-law: (if living)	Name _____
	Name _____
	Name _____
	Name _____

Cousins:	Name _____
	Name _____
	Name _____

Nieces and nephews:	Name _____
	Name _____
	Name _____

Grandchildren: Name _____

                        Name _____

                        Name _____

                        Name _____

Your aunts and uncles: Name _____

  (*still living*)   Name _____

                        Name _____

                        Name _____

                        Name _____

Go back and place a check (✔)next to the names of those that you feel very close to. Go back again and place an asterisk (*) next to the names of those you do not feel close to. Go back again and circle the asterisk (✱) next to the names of those you do not feel close to, but wish you did.

B. Friends

In your notebook, write out your definition of "friend." Then, using your definition of friend, write the first names of your very best friends in the spaces provided below and check the appropriate squares.

Name	Family	Work/School	Church	Neighborhood	Older Than You	Same Age	Younger Than You	Makes More $	Makes Same $	Makes Less $	Professed Christian	Together Last

1. Place an "X" in the appropriate space if the person is a family member.
2. Place an "X" in the appropriate space if the person is involved with you in your work, is present at your place of employment, or attends your school.
3. Place an "X" in the appropriate space if the person attends your church.
4. Place an "X" in the appropriate space if the person lives in your neighborhood.
5. Place an "X" in AGE category that best describes the situation: "+" if the person is older than you, "S" if the person is about the same age, "-" if the person is younger than you.
6. Place an "X" if the INCOME category that best describes the situation: "+" if the person has more income, "S" if the person has approximately the same income, "-" if the person has less income.
7. Place an "X" in the appropriate space if the person is a professed Christian.
8. In the appropriate space, jot down the date of the last time you were together with the person.

In your notebook list the three people (not necessarily in sequential order) whom you really have a tough time accepting.

C. Influence

Influence is a strange possession. It is your ability to affect others around you.
- How many people would you guess to be within the circle of your influence?
  ☐ 0-50   ☐ 1,000-10,000
  ☐ 50-100   ☐ More than 10,000
  ☐ 100-1,000

- If everyone within the circle of your influence were asked to use *one word* to best describe your influence on them, what *one word* would most often be used?

- What one word do *you wish* would be most often used?

IV. SPIRITUAL POSSESSIONS

Read entirely through the list below. Then go back and, on a scale of 1-10 (1 being low . . . 10 being high), rate yourself according to your own spiritual qualities.
1. _____ I am genuinely kind to others.
2. _____ I have good self-control.

3. _____ I put others first.
4. _____ I am at peace with myself.
5. _____ I am at peace with others.
6. _____ I have a meaningful and satisfying relationship with Christ.
7. _____ I can genuinely love others.
8. _____ It's easy to give generously to my family.
9. _____ It's easy to give generously to others.
10. _____ My life is characterized by a deep joy.
11. _____ I am patient with those in my family.
12. _____ I am patient with others.
13. _____ I am genuinely a good person.
14. _____ My life is characterized by consistency.
15. _____ I am faithful; you can count on me.
16. _____ I find it easy not to harbor grudges.
17. _____ I can take criticism well.
18. _____ I have a noncomplaining attitude.
19. _____ I find it easy to forgive others.
20. _____ I am happy with what I have and don't get upset over what others have.

V. SPECIAL POSSESSIONS

In addition to all of your other possessions, God has given to you some special talents or abilities. You may have refined them and put a lot of practice and discipline into their development, but you realize that they are special possessions given to you by a discerning God. In your notebook list your special talents and abilities.

Go back and place a star (☆) beside the ones that you feel are your strongest talents or abilities. Are those the areas that would best represent your personal likes and dislikes?

3

Your Personal Inheritance

No doubt as you went through the exercise of listing your possessions in the previous chapter, you had some mixed feelings. Probably you were a little surprised that you possess as much as you do. Perhaps you had fun reliving some of the particular experiences connected with your collection of unique possessions. Things may have even gotten a little serious when you were dealing with your spiritual possessions or your limited possession of time.

However, in a study such as this, there is one question that jumps up and demands to be answered: "How'd you get what'cha got?"

Black's Law Dictionary by Henry Campbell Black (St. Paul: West Publishing Co., 1951) describes "estate" as . . . comprehend(ing) every species of property, real and personal (p. 643). "Inheritance" is defined as: An *estate* in things . . . descending to the heir (p. 922). Therefore, quite simply stated, your inheritance is everything you have received from someone else.

Stop for a moment and consider again those things you listed previously in your portfolio of possessions. What possessions which you now enjoy *did not* ultimately originate as a gift to you?

I. FACTORS THAT INFLUENCE YOUR INHERITANCE

A. The Gift Exchange

When asked the question, "How'd you get what'cha got?" you may have replied rather quickly, "The old-fashioned way. I earned it."

You are to be commended for your industry! But, more precisely it could be stated that you traded for all your acquired possessions. When you get up in the morning and go to work for that favorite employer of yours, you simply trade your skills and time for something known as a paycheck which in turn you take to the bank and trade for cash, which in turn you trade for things you want and need.

But as you tract the steps backward, you still come again to the ultimate question of where you got the basic commodities that you trade for the things you want and need. Reduced to their lowest common denominator, those basic commodities which you use as trading material for everything else were given to you!

- You did not purchase your time allotment which you now hold as a possession. *It was given to you.*
- You did not negotiate for your physical characteristics. *You inherited them.*
- You did not bargain on the open market for your basic intellectual capacities. *You received them as a gift.*
- You did not ardently go to battle and finally win the power to choose. *That power was given to you.*
- Even the environment in which you move and perform your trading activities came to you as *part of your inheritance.*

It is of extreme importance to recognize that everything you now possess was received directly as a gift or *a by-product of a gift exchange.*

One of the often overlooked phrases used in Christ's parable of the "Talents" (Mt. 25:14-30) reveals the true origin of all possessions: To one *He gave* five talents. To one *He gave* two. To one *He gave* one. Ultimately, there is only one source of all possessions, one "sole proprietor" of all that exists whether ordinary or yet to be discovered. That one sole proprietor is Jehovah God—"Yahweh"—the Giver of every good and perfect gift.

The apostle Paul posed a penetrating question to his friends in Corinth: "What do you have that God hasn't given you?" (I Cor. 4:7b, TLB).

B. The Agency Agreement

An *agent* is a person authorized by another to act for him, one entrusted with another's business who undertakes to manage the affair and to render to him an account thereof. This is what Christ was talking about in John's Gospel when He said, "I appointed you to go and produce lovely fruit always, so that no matter what you ask for from the Father, *using my name*, he will give it to you" (Jn. 15:16, TLB, emphasis added). The term "using my name" is like a "power of attorney" to do as His agent what He would *do, say,* and *request if He were here personally.*

An agency relationship has been established between Christ and us, and we are to carry out *Christ's will* here on earth just as if He were here, Himself, in person! However, using that "power of attorney" to acquire things that *Christ would not have asked for* could result in our being charged with *forgery*. The whole idea is mind stretching! Think of all of this in relationship to your own personal inheritance—all those things that you have in your portfolio of possessions. There is a tremendous responsibility that goes along with those possessions.

C. The Trust Account

Is it possible that *all* that we possess has been given to us and we are simply trustees? Was it all deposited in our trust accounts to be distributed out to others in order to benefit the Kingdom of God?

I went to *Black's Law Dictionary* by Henry Campbell Black (St. Paul: West Publishing Co., 1951) to find out for myself. I looked under "trust" (p. 1620) and found the following.

> TRUST: A right of property, real or personal, held by one party for the benefit of another. A confidence reposed in one person, who is termed *trustee*, for the benefit of another. . . . Any arrangement whereby property is *transferred with intention that it be administered by trustee for another's benefit.*

The concept began to come into focus. Was it really possible that all those things listed in my portfolio of possessions were placed there by God, either directly or through a gift exchange, not for my enjoyment alone, *but for the benefit of others*? I then went to God's Word and found: "You will be made rich in every way *so that* you can be generous on every occasion . . ." (II Cor. 9:11, NIV, emphasis added). I took special note of the "*so that*," which revealed the true motivation behind why God makes us rich. This was really starting to make sense!

Back into the *Black's Law Dictionary* (p. 1680):

> TRUST (continued): . . . An *obligation* on a person arising out of confidence reposed in him to apply property faithfully and according to such confidence; as being in nature of deposition by which proprietor transfers to another party of subject intrusted, *not that it should remain with him, but that it should be applied to certain uses for the behoof of third party.*

I didn't know a person could get blessed by reading a law dictionary! Then I was reminded that this was not an option but a mandate. It talked of *obligation* and *confidence*. Just think of it! God has enough confidence in us to entrust us with everything we possess.

So God created man in his own image, in the image of God created he him; male and female created he them. And God blessed them, and God said unto them, Be fruitful, and multiply, and replenish the earth, and subdue it: and have dominion over the fish of the sea, and over the fowl of the air, and over every living thing that moveth upon the earth (Gen. 1:27-28, KJV).

Consider for a moment the confidence that God expressed in you, when He deposited your inheritance into your trust account believing that you would respond to that arrangement as a "trustworthy administrator." He is counting on you as an integral part of His plan for meeting the needs of others around you. If you fail in your trustee responsibility, the whole plan suffers. But as you faithfully respond and others faithfully respond, then God's plan has a chance to function efficiently. As the diagram shows, everyone receives some things directly from God, but many benefits must be passed on from fellow trustees. That's God's plan.

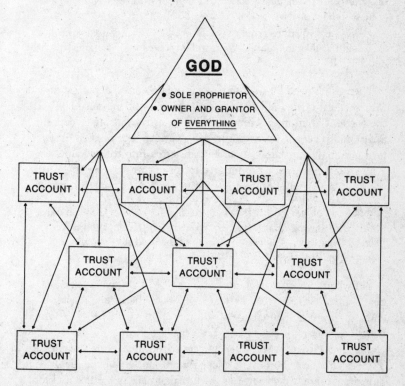

"GOD TO PEOPLE... PEOPLE TO PEOPLE"

II. PRACTICAL PRINCIPLES PERTAINING TO YOUR PERSONAL POSSESSIONS

1. *The sum total of your possessions that you identified in chapter two is the current inventory of your trust account and is there as a result of a direct gift or a gift exchange.*
2. *The inventory in your trust account is to be administered by you, the trustee, for the benefit of others.*
3. *As you, the trustee, transfer inventory out of your trust account into the trust accounts of others, God makes compensating deposits into your trust account . . . thus allowing you to give even more into the trust accounts of others.*

Consider these verses:

Now it is required that those who have been given a trust must prove faithful (I Cor. 4:2, NIV).

For the man who uses well what he is given shall be given more, and he shall have abundance (Mt. 25:29a, TLB).

Give, and it will be given to you. A good measure, pressed down, shaken together and running over, will be poured into your lap (Lk. 6:38a, NIV).

There is no need for God to make a compensating deposit into your trust account until you have made a trust account transfer (TAT) into the account of another. However, God is *eagerly* waiting to deposit additional inventory into your trust account, not to be used for your own personal gain, but to *again* be transferred into the accounts of others. Remember, you do not give to get or transfer your inventory with the intention of forcing or tricking God into giving you more:

You can be sure of this: The kingdom of Christ and of God will never belong to anyone who is impure or greedy, for a greedy person is really an idol worshiper—he loves and worships the good things of this life more than God (Eph. 5:5, TLB).

But when your trust account transfers (TAT) are made out of a heart of *thanksgiving* and an attitude of *praise*, the compensating consequence is an abundance of additional inventory being deposited back into your trust account! A few years ago Annie and I were challenged with an interesting concept: tithe your estate now, or TYEN. There was nothing particularly brilliant about the idea. However, there *was* something about it that caught our imagination. As far as I knew, I had paid tithe on every "dollar" I had ever earned from childhood, even during the years that we were away from the church. However, there were equities and properties that we had accumulated that had come through trades and had not included cash "dollars" at all; therefore, no tithe had been paid. And there were equities that had appreciated in value. When would we ever pay tithe on these? If we waited until we died, the local, state, and federal governments would have taken the largest portion of the estate. Besides, wouldn't it be fun to see the money at work in God's Kingdom business while we were still alive? We accepted the challenge and decided to go for it!

However, when Annie and I had figured out how much money we needed to come up with for our TYEN, it was a lot of cash. We pulled from savings, sold some things, but we were still $30,000 *short!* How were we ever going to do it?

One morning I was standing in front of our home, subconsciously watching the reflection of the clouds in the calm water of the lake, but consciously quizzing God on how I was ever going to follow through on the balance of my commitment to TYEN. Then my attention seemed to shift from the lake to two Swiss chalets on the property adjacent to ours. They were beautiful—looked like they had just come off a travel postcard. They had been built by Mrs. Cannon of the "Gates Rubber" family, but for 11 years no one had lived in them or even visited except to maintain them. God seemed to assure me that our answer would be provided through those two adjacent properties.

The next Sunday afternoon, as we turned our car into the driveway, we noticed smoke coming out of one of the large stone fireplaces. Who could be in there? Perhaps someone had broken in! we thought. We quietly walked up close enough to the house to see that there were several people in the house having what seemed to be a party. We quickly returned to our house and called the Mountain Parks Protective Association.

However, by late afternoon when we were ready to return to church the patrol had still not arrived. So we called the sheriff. As we were pulling out of the driveway, the sheriff arrived—hand on gun—and assured us he'd take care of everything.

But Monday morning we got a call from an irate manager of the Mountain Parks Protective Association asking why we went over his head to bring in the sheriff. "That made us look bad. Those people in there were the grandkids of old Mrs. Cannon. They were up there going through all the stuff, taking what they wanted . . . now that the old lady is dead."

I don't remember now if I said "good-bye" or not, because I was on my way down to the bank to see Joe Chamberlain, the fellow who was handling the Cannon estate.

"Mr. Chamberlain," I said, "I would like to buy both of the Cannon houses."

"Both of them? Why?"

"Well, they are contiguous to our property. Besides, we have something in mind for them."

A few weeks later, Joe called and informed me that he had received several offers on the houses individually, but since I had wanted both, it would be simpler to let me have them in a package deal.

We cleaned out all the beautiful antiques, put down new carpeting, and ordered an appraisal for a new mortgage. Would you believe? At 75 percent of the appraised value, we were able to borrow exactly $30,000 *more than what we paid!* Since then, the tenants' rent has covered every one of the mortgage payments (and then some). I'll never forget the feeling of walking up and giving that $30,000 check to my pastor and hazily becoming aware of the concept that, as you transfer inventory out of your trust account into the trust accounts of others, God makes compensating deposits into your trust account . . . thus allowing you to give even more into the trust accounts of others.

4. *God determines the AMOUNT, KIND, and TIMING of the compensating deposits. The trustee is only responsible for the current inventory in the account.*

Many people through the years have become disillusioned and, in some cases, bitter, because they tried to dictate to God the amount, kind, and timing of the compensating deposit. They had it figured that if they gave $100 toward a missionary project, then God would be obligated to compensate by depositing $1,000 in cash back into their account by Christmastime. It is certainly possible that He might! But on the other hand, He just might *NOT!* He just might have had a creative plan in mind that necessitated a different kind of possession to be deposited in their account that would aid the advancement of His kingdom far more than cold cash. Their disillusionment came because their own expectations limited their awareness of God's creative method of making compensating deposits. Remember, "If you are really eager to give, then it isn't important how much you have to give. God wants you to give what you have, not what you haven't" (II Cor. 8:12, TLB).

5. *God has guaranteed to take care of all your personal needs as trustee as long as you are faithfully administering your trust account.*

Day by day the Lord observes the good deeds done by godly men, and gives them eternal rewards. He cares for them when times are hard; even in famine, they will have enough. I have been young and now I am old. And in all my years I have never seen the Lord forsake a man who loves him; nor have I seen the children of the godly go hungry. Instead, the godly are able to be generous with their gifts and loans to others, and their children are a blessing (Ps. 37:18, 19, 25, 26, TLB).

6. A neglected opportunity for a trust account transfer (TAT) negates the necessity of a compensating deposit.

It is possible to give away and become richer! *It is also possible to hold on too tightly and lose everything.* Yes, the liberal man shall be rich! By watering others, he waters himself (Prov. 11:24, 25, TLB).

7. As a faithful trustee, your trust account is guaranteed never to be declared "bankrupt."

The Lord will give you an abundance of good things in the land, just as he promised: many children, many cattle, and abundant crops. He will open to you his wonderful treasury of rain in the heavens, to give you fine crops every season. He will bless everything you do; and you shall lend to many nations (Deut. 28:11-13, TLB).

But my God shall supply all your need according to his riches in glory by Christ Jesus (Phil. 4:19, KJV).

8. Deposited into your trust account is exactly what someone around you needs.

Tell those who are rich not to be proud and not to trust in their money, which will soon be gone, but their pride and trust should be in the living God who always richly gives us all we need for our enjoyment. Tell them to use their money to do good. They should be rich in good works *and should give happily to those in need, always being ready to share with others whatever God has given them* (I Tim. 6:17, 18, TLB, emphasis added).

. . . but you should divide with them. Right now you have plenty and can help them; then at some other time they can share with you when you need it. In this way each will have as much as he needs (II Cor. 8:14, TLB).

How is your sensitivity level to God's will as it relates to the needs of those around you? Stop now and ask the Holy Spirit to help match up the inventory in your trust account with the needs of those around you. What do you have that God would like for you to share with someone else? What could you transfer from your trust account into his or her trust account? Perhaps it will be an invitation to your house for dinner, or to a restaurant for breakfast. Perhaps you need to call someone to give him a few words of encouragement. Maybe there is something in your trust account that seems rather insignificant to you but is exactly what that other person needs.

After you have had some time to meditate, write down in your notebook your intentions. For each item, use the following format:

I need to transfer _____ *into the*
(Possession)

trust account of _____
(Name of person)

I can accomplish this by _____
(Action to be taken)

With God's help I will do it by _____
(Date)

This is an important part of God's plan for meeting the needs of His children. Part of the inventory in your trust account is your *special abilities*. You must be sensitive to the opportunities to share these abilities with others around you.

> However, Christ has given each of us special abilities—whatever he wants us to have out of his rich storehouse of gifts. Under his direction the whole body is fitted together perfectly, *and each part in its own special way helps the other parts,* so that the whole body is healthy and growing and full of love (Eph. 4:7, 16, TLB, emphasis added).

Let me suggest that for the next four weeks, you become involved in the trust account transfer (TAT) system. Try using *Transfer Slips* as you transfer something from your trust account to the trust account of someone else. It is up to you to determine the type of transfer. For example, you may want to bake some cinnamon rolls or a batch of cookies for your recipient. When you make your delivery, you simply write out a transfer slip and place it on the plate with the goodies, give it to them, smile, and tell them you just wanted to do it for them. If they can't figure out what's gotten into you and inquire about the transfer slip, you may wish to take the opportunity to explain to them what you have been learning about *sharing.* If they insist on trying to reciprocate, ask them to simply pass on a good deed to someone else that week. (They will be trying to answer the personal question, "What'cha gonna do with what'cha got?")

If you can't bake goodies, you may want to try something else, e.g., pick up someone's car and have it washed, buy a plant for someone's office, offer to take care of a couple's kids without charge so they can have a night (or weekend) out, send a "care package" to someone at college, offer to let someone use your cabin on the lake.

Remember, don't concern yourself with the possibility of any compensating balance. That's not your problem. Your concern is with transferring things out of your trust account into the trust account of others. Start making TATs a way of life.

9. If you selfishly hoard that which has been deposited into your trust account, it will become "miser's manna" and will rot!

> For unless you are honest in small matters, you won't be in large ones. If you cheat even a little, you won't be honest with greater responsibilities. And if you are *untrustworthy* about worldly wealth, who will trust you with the true riches of heaven? (Lk. 16:10, 11, TLB, emphasis added).

Do you recall the interesting episode that occurred during the exodus of Moses and the children of Israel? God had promised that He would provide for His people. When they were thirsty, God had Moses strike the rock with that humble rod, and water poured out. When the people became hungry, God produced a phenomenal product called "manna" which looked a lot like early morning frost and tasted like honey bread. God instructed them that they did not need to be apprehensive about the sufficiency of the Source or greedy in their gathering. God assured them that there would always be enough to meet their needs.

However, taking God at His word doesn't always seem to be the natural course for mankind. Sure enough, their fears found them fetching and hoarding more than the needed. And when they went back to their hoarded treasure, they found not *manna*, but *only mildew and maggots.*

10. As a result of a trust account transfer (TAT), two things happen: needs are met and God is praised.

> For God, who gives seed to the farmer to plant, and later on, good crops to harvest and eat, will give you more and more seed to plant and will make it grow *so that* you can give away more and more fruit from your harvest.
>
> Yes, God will give you much *so that* you can give away much, and when we take your gifts to those who need them they will break out into thanksgiving and praise to God for your help.
>
> So, *two good things happen as a result of your gifts*—those in need are helped, and they overflow with thanks to God. Those you help will be glad not only because of your generous gifts to themselves and to others, but they will praise God for this proof that your deeds are as good as your doctrine. And they will pray for you with deep fervor and feeling because of the wonderful grace of God shown through you (II Cor. 9:10-14, TLB, emphasis added).

As you begin, out of your inventory, to share with those around you, their needs are met. As they begin to share their ministry with those around the, your needs are met. Each time there is a trust account transfer (TAT), there is an opportunity for true worship to take place. *Praise* will *go to God when* you fully *recognize Him for who He is . . . the true Source, the Giver of every good and perfect gift.*

I have no complaint about the sacrifices you bring to my altar, for you bring them regularly. But it isn't sacrificial bullocks and goats that I really want from you. For all the animals of field and forest are mine! The cattle on a thousand hills! And all the birds upon the mountains! If I was hungry, I would not mention it to you—*for all the world is mine, and everything in it.* No, I don't need your sacrifices of flesh and blood. *What I want from you is your true thanks; I want your promises fulfilled. I want you to trust me in your times of trouble, so I can rescue you, and you can give me glory* (Ps. 50:8-15, TLB, emphasis added).

Paul states in II Corinthians 9:11 that who receive a gift will break out into *thanksgiving* and *praise* and that there will be an overflowing of thanks to God. This act of true worship takes place on both ends of the transfer. The one who receives has an occasion to praise God. But likewise, the one who had just been afforded the opportunity to give, also discovers a rewarding dimension of thanks.

But wait a minute. There is a *third* result mentioned in the Scripture: "*And they will pray for you* with deep fervor and feeling because of the wonderful grace of God shown through you" II Cor. 9:14, TLB, emphasis added. In the business world you would call this a "To Boot" or a "Kicker" or something extra special that you did not expect! They will pray for you. Not only will needs be met and God be praised, but you will be honored by the prayers of those who recognize that you are fitting into God's plan and economy.

III. POSSESSIVENESS VERSUS RELINQUISHMENT

From research into God's Word and from continued observation of human behavior, I believe that *one can safely conclude that the chief natural characteristic of humans is possessiveness.*

Possessiveness is the attitude and activity of selfishly holding on to those things that are included in your trust account inventory. Sin has complicated the trust account concept. Greed has transformed the gifts into a grotesque source for potential ruin. Satan very subtly seduces us into becoming unfaithful trustees. By simple rationalization, we fraudulently fail in our responsibilities.

Fraud is a strong word. What does it mean? *Black's Law Dictionary* (page 788) says:

. . . a generic term, embracing all multifarious means which human ingenuity can devise, and which are resorted to by one individual to get advantage over another by false suggestions or by suppression of truth, and includes all surprise, trick or cunning dissembling, and any unfair way *by which another is cheated.*

"*Bad Faith*" and "*Fraud*" are synonymous and also synonyms of *dishonesty, infidelity, faithlessness, perfidy, unfairness,* etc. . . . And includes anything calculated to deceive, whether it be a single act or combination of circumstances, whether the suppression of truth or the suggestion of what is false, whether it be by direct falsehood or by innuendo, by speech or by silence, by word of mouth, or by look or gesture.

When a *trustee* who is holding a possession in his *inventory* that was intended for the benefit of a third party fails to surrender that possession and instead retains that inventory for his own gratification, it is possible that the unfaithful trustee might be guilty of *fraud.*

On the other hand, there is a *blessedness of trusteeship* where we are no longer slaves to the tyranny of things. There is a spirit of relinquishment that enables the breaking of oppressor's yoke, not through hoarding, but through *surrender.* I like the word "relinquish." It recognizes the fact that I have the right to have or possess something *but* that I intentionally abandon, surrender, give up, and bind over to someone else that which I have.

Christ continually taught that we are victorious through surrender, that we win through relinquishment.

> If any man will come after me, let him deny himself, and take up his cross, and follow me. For whosoever will save his life shall lose it: and whosoever will lose his life for my sake shall find it (Mt. 16:24b, 25, KJV).

As is so frequently the case, this New Testament principle of spiritual life finds an excellent illustration in the Old Testament. The story of Abraham and Isaac is a classic portrayal of *relinquishment.*

God had promised Abraham that he and Sarah would have a son and that through that son, his descendants would be multiplied into countless numbers, like the stars in the sky. Abraham believed God. But Abraham was 100 years old and Sarah was 90 before God fulfilled His promise through the birth of Isaac. What a precious possession to be placed in Abraham's trust account!

As Abraham watched Isaac grow, he felt a love bond develop that he had never before known. Day after day their lives were being knitted together like the flawless fabric of a beautiful garment. But when Isaac was about 36 years old, God began to engineer an experience that would result in *relinquishment.*

> Take with you your only son—yes, Isaac whom you love so much— and go to the land of Moriah and sacrifice him there as a burnt offering

upon one of the mountains which I'll point out to you! (Gen. 22:2, TLB).

The Scripture is kind and spares us from the agony of witnessing Abraham throughout that long, dark night. There he fought the battle of his life on the field of his own possessions. But as the first splinters of gray dawn began piercing holes in the black shroud of that eastern night, Abraham arose and began preparing for the trip— wood, flint, servants, donkey . . . *Isaac*.

They traveled for three days. Then requesting that the others stay behind, Abraham and his son went on to the top of the mountain. "Father . . . we have the wood and the flint to make the fire, but where is the lamb for the sacrifice?" asked Isaac. *"God will see to it, my son. . . ."*

The writer of Hebrews tells us that Abraham was so convinced of God's integrity that he believed, if necessary, God would raise Isaac from the dead.

> He built an altar and placed the wood in order, ready for the fire, and then tied Isaac and laid him on the altar over the wood. And Abraham took the knife and lifted it up to plunge it into his son, to slay him (vss. 9, 10).

God allowed the suffering old patriarch to go through with the experience up to the point where He knew there would be no retreat, and then commanded him: *"Lay down the knife; don't hurt the lad in any way"* (vs. 12).

God had no intention of allowing Abraham to bring harm to his beloved Isaac. But through this experience, he was leading Abraham into an experience of relinquishment where the power of possessiveness could be paralyzed and he could render up a sweet sacrifice of total surrender. God said, "For I know that God is first in your life—you have not withheld even your beloved son from me" (vs. 12).

I'm sure Abraham and Isaac stood there on top of Mount Moriah that day, locked in a silent embrace for a long time. Tears of triumph no doubt coursed down the cheeks of both the old patriarch and the young man. But they were proven trustworthy trustees of all that God had given them.

As they walked back down off the mountain that day, where years later the beautiful city of Jerusalem would stand, Abraham had his arm around the shoulders of Isaac. He could see clearly now. Everything that had ever been entrusted to him was still his to enjoy . . . but now it was different, *really different*.

4

Your Economic Inheritance

We are still dealing with the question of "How'd you get what'cha got?" As you worked you way through Chapter Three, you were reminded of the fact that everything you now possess came to you as part of your personal inheritance. But there is something that must be further understood at this point which greatly affects your "Portfolio of Possessions." *You were born into a system of economic thought and activity that continually influences you and your decisions.*

One afternoon a man came huffing and puffing into his house, slammed the door, and fell exhausted into a living room chair. He was met there by his wife: "What's wrong? Why are you so out of breath?"

"I know you'll be proud of me! I *ran* all the way home from work . . . behind the bus . . . and I saved 30¢!"

"You are so stupid. You are so dumb, dumb, dumb! If you were going to run all the way home, why didn't you run behind a taxi and save $3.00?"

However well you understand the workings of the economic system, you must always remember that this economic structure in which you live and operate is part of your basic inheritance.

I. ECONOMIC TRADITION

In 336 B.C., a 21 year old was placed on the Greek throne following the assassination of his father, Philip. Alexander of Macedonia had been schooled at the feet of Aristotle who had made him aware of a world that was fragmented economically into countless little city-states, each with its own government, money system, army, and customs. He realized the high cost of fragmentation and, in the next dozen years, Alexander the Great "conquered" the world for Greece. He conquered it with such interesting subtlety that more often than not, the countries in his path simply threw open their gates and welcomed him. He brought with him *security, protection,* and *fairness,* and he encouraged free trade within his world based on a dependable metallic coinage of gold and silver. The genius of that economic unification rested in the fact that it did not cost his constituents more for those additional benefits, but less . . . a whole lot less.

Where the citizens had been paying as much as 70 to 80 percent in taxes to operate their fragmented city-states, Alexander reduced those tax rates to around 15 percent. Little wonder that they threw open their gates and welcomed him with open arms!

But alas, with no more worlds to conquer, Alexander the Great died at the age of 33 as a result of a wild drinking party. The insecure European and Asian populace then moved back toward the mass of fragmented city-states, no longer unified by protection and a stable economy. His empire crumbled, but his dream lived on.

Two hundred seventy-one years later, Julius Caesar laid claim to Alexander's dream, overhauled it, and began to implement the great experiment: *Pax Romana.* The global economy was not nearly as fragmented as it had been prior to Alexander, and the Greek philosophy, literature, and ideas of democracy had done much to break down the barriers between the Greeks and the barbarians.

Julius Caesar, like Alexander, began building his empire, not primarily through brutal conquest but rather through economic and political *liberation.* Five years after he had taken over Gaul, Julius Caesar entered Italy, where Rome opened her gates and welcomed him as her new champion and leader. He made the stability of the Roman currency so attractive, the mildness of Roman taxation so alluring, the openness of worldwide trade and commerce so desirable that his empire expanded by the force of demand. He treated the "conquered" nations with such secure leniency, that even if they could have revolted, they didn't! The economy began to grow, trade began to flourish, the Roman Empire was established. Julius Caesar perceived that individual initiative and creativity that was *rewarded* produced more individual initiative and more creativity—thus a more stable and wealthy empire. He also perceived that exorbitant taxation squelched individual initiative and creativity. He therefore set out on a plan to broaden the tax base so that he could lower the individual tax rate, i.e., include more people on the tax rolls but lower the amount that each had to pay on his production so that they would be encouraged to produce more, thereby making the empire wealthier and all the people happier. In order to do this, he needed to take a census of the empire. He was able to see his plan only partially fulfilled. A census was taken of Italy only.

In 44 B.C. Julius Caesar was brutally assassinated by aristocratic friends who wanted him not to forget that he was still human. But in those eight years (52-44 B.C.), Julius Caesar had established an economic/political system that endured for the next 500 years and is still influencing the American experiment even today.

After 16 years of civil war, Octavius, the adopted son of Julius Caesar, desirous of fulfilling his father's plan, victoriously returned to Rome as Caesar Augustus, Emperor of Rome. Does that name sound familiar? It should. Does a census for taxation ring a bell? It should: "And it came to pass in those days, that there went out a decree from Caesar Augustus, that all the world should be taxed" (Lk. 2:1, KJV).

Julius Caesar had passed on to his adopted son his dream for the economic empire. And Caesar Augustus, carrying out his father's plan, created the stable setting into which the King of Kings and Lord of Lords was born. In Galatians 4:4 we read, "When the fulness of the time was come, God sent forth his Son" (KJV). Isn't it amazing that God used the political security of a global economy as a vehicle for the spreading of the Gospel story?

If given opportunity, this economic phenomenon could be pursued through the historic chapters of Napoleon, the rise of the English Empire (Pax Britannica), and the grand experiment of Revolutionary America. Perhaps the most influential economic work of the 18th century was *Wealth of Nations*, written by the Scottish economist Adam Smith (1793-90), explaining the principles of capitalism and free enterprise. He believed that governments should not interfere with economic competition and free trade which was necessary for strong economic growth. Smith had a tremendous influence on the Revolutionary fathers of young America.

The most influential economic work of the 19th century was *Das Kapital*, by the German philosopher Karl Marx (1818-83), explaining the principles of collective communism. Marx disagreed with Smith and argued that the only solution to the class struggle between worker and employer was for the government to own everything and totally control distribution.

Without being too simplistic, all economic/political systems being carried out by nations today are divided at the point of income growth versus income redistribution. The tensions between those two camps of economic thought are the fundamental reasons for the political experiments of the last 200 years.

Capitalistic economies as seen at work in the United States and Canada have been primarily concerned with economic *growth* and expansion with a heavy emphasis on the freedoms of the individual. Communistic economies, experimented with by China and Russia, are primarily concerned with *distribution* of activities and products with a heavy emphasis on the powers of the government.

How has Christianity survived all of this economic tension over the past 2,000 years? Contrary to Marx's conclusion that it is the "opiate of the masses," and contrary to Voltaire's view that the political class uses religion as a means of pacifying the mob, Christianity has been the historic "Epoxy" that has held the world together over the past centuries. The church as an institution has been able to adjust to a needy world supporting *growth* and the individual freedom in the good times, and supporting *redistribution* in the bad times. Further, Christianity has been vigorously evangelical and open to anyone and has always insisted on its disciples seriously facing the question: "What'cha gonna do with what'cha got?"

II. WHAT IS ECONOMICS?

The word "economics" is derived from the Greek words *oikos* (a house) and *nemein* (to manage), and quite simply deals with *why* and *how* people *produce, distribute,* and *consume* goods and services. The very term "economics" frightens many people. They feel that they know absolutely *nothing* about the subject and that there is no hope of ever learning! Quite the contrary is true! Individuals are exposed to the basic principles of economics from the *cradle*, and by the age of six or seven, the child has learned the principles and has probably a degree of sophistication in applying them. At a very, very early age a child begins to communicate *what* he or she has to *produce*, *what* he or she wants to *consume*, *when* and under *what conditions* he or she is *willing to trade*. The principle of supply and demand is experienced and well understood while still in the nursery. The child needs a supply of food and does not hesitate to make his demands known to the mother, who can supply the demands. The mother is willing and eager to enter into an agreement to meet the demands of the child out of her supply. The demands are met, and both parties are happy with the deal. The child begins to understand that in any economic transaction there must be at least two people involved: 1. a "demander" (consumer); 2. a "supplier" (producer).

A little later the child learns that there are terms of trade that have to be negotiated and agreed upon. In the nursery scene the child was not only the "demander" but also a "supplier." The mother was not only the "supplier" but she was a "demander." Furthermore, these roles functioned at the same time. For instance, 1. The child *demanded* to be fed but could *supply* peace and quiet. 2. The mother could *supply* the food but *demanded* peace and quiet. The *terms of the trade* were: food exchanged for peace and quiet.

Soon the child recognizes that he has other marketable products, e.g., display of love and affection. He begins to work on his portfolio of marketable products. A big smile and a cooing sound is a highly marketable item and is easily traded for favorable attention. He finds that reaching his arms out and happily going to other people is a very desirable commodity and *expands his marketplace* for favors. He increases the *appreciation level* for his peace and quiet product by perfecting a counterbalancing product . . . crying and screaming.

It really isn't long at all until the child learns that if he wants something from someone, something must be traded in return, and those two somethings must be roughly of equal value because, in a successful voluntary exchange, both sides must benefit.

When the time comes for changing a diaper, the child becomes aware of another interesting principle: price is a *ratio* of product values and not just a single number. The child is very willing to supply peace and quiet, but only if he can get rid of that smelly diaper!

Where's Mother? Can't she understand? But alas! She is in the kitchen talking with one of her friends . . . drinking a cup of coffee. The child is suddenly introduced to the concept of *competition*, others vying for her product of attention. It's not that Mother is unwilling to supply the clean diaper, but the *terms of trade* must be reestablished and the price must be renegotiated. The child begins to make his demands known and at the same time builds in *an appreciation* for his supply of peace and quiet. By the time the diaper is changed, he has discovered that the price of a clean diaper is two whimpers, four cries, and two screams. The price was simply a *ratio* of products.

When the child is older he or she discovers some new levels of economic negotiations: "If you will clean up your bedroom, I'll let you stay up and watch TV." The child has to *invest* in producing the product of a clean bedroom on the *promise* that Mother will allow staying up late to watch TV. Now the child begins to understand credit. Credit is simply the *promise to pay* upon the receipt of the goods.

Let's say at this point that the child decides to test the *stability of the monetary system*.

"Okay, Mom! You can come and inspect my room. I'm done."

"But, the bed is not made. Just look! Instead of picking up your clothes and hanging them neatly in the closet, you just threw them all in the dirty clothes basket. But that's okay, honey. You did pretty well. You can still stay up and watch TV."

The monetary standard has just declined! The system has just experienced *inflation*. Since the *same reward* was made available for the purchase of *less product*, a new *value* will be placed on that product. From that point on, it will cost her more than the amount of the old reward to get the room cleaned *properly*.

The child may decide to clean the room properly, as agreed at the beginning, but elect to use the mother's credit promise as *money*. Money is simply a credit instrument. It has a recognized standard value and can be easily exchanged for something in the future. The child might say, "Mom, I'll clean my bedroom but I would rather *not* stay up and watch TV. I would rather have that model racing car down at the drugstore." He has now been able to use the credit instrument (money) for something he would rather have.

The child may forego the present consumption of the credit in hopes that he will be able to consume at a later date. "Mom, I'll keep my bedroom spotless for six months for that fancy Mongoose bike down at the Schwinn shop." This is simply called *capital investment* where he gives up current consumption with the anticipation of consuming in the future. (Do you remember the tremendous *capital investment* that Jacob made for Rachel? Gen. 29.)

Before very long the child learns something else about the principle of supply and demand: *supply always equals demand*. Suppose: "Hey, Joey! I'll trade you my two plastic model airplanes for five of your baseball trading cards you got out of the bubble gum packages."

It was stated earlier that everyone is a supplier *and* a demander . . . at the same time. Here our little friend has a *supply* (supplier) of plastic model planes, and he *wants* (demander) some baseball cards. Joey has a *supply* (supplier) of baseball cards and *maybe wants* (potential demander) the model planes. If they agree on the terms of trade, they make a deal. But even if they *don't* make the trade, supply still equals demand because they each demanded *their own supply* more than the other's. Joey ended up demanding *his own* supply of five baseball cards, and our little friend ended up demanding *his own* supply of two model planes. *Therefore, a trade is not required for supply to equal demand.*

Market price is established at whatever point Joey desires his own baseball cards *less* than he desires the model planes—or—he may demand some *additional quantity* of model planes to equal his baseball cards. Maybe the *market price* will be three planes instead of two, or two planes for four baseball cards instead of five.

Again: *by the time a child is six or seven years old, he or she has learned the basic economic principles and has probably developed a degree of sophistication in applying them.* How then does all of this fit into the national economy that you have received as part of your inheritance?

III. A WHIRLWIND VIEW OF ECONOMICS

This is a hot dog. It is called a **PRODUCT.**

It consists of a bun,
　　　　　a wiener,
　　　　　catsup,
　　　　　relish,
　　　　　mustard.

They are **RAW MATERIALS.**

Eddy Entrepreneur put all these raw materials together to make the product. Eddy is a **PRODUCER.**

Polly Purchaser wants to buy one of Eddy's hot dogs. Polly is a **CONSUMER.**

If Eddy allows Polly to buy one of the hot dogs, the transaction is called a **SALE.**

The amount that Polly pays for the hot dog is called the **PRICE.**

The instrument Polly uses to pay for the hot dog is called **MONEY.**

Because Polly is willing to pay the price that Eddy is asking, they have established **MARKET VALUE.**

If no one else is selling hot dogs, Eddy has a **MONOPOLY.**

If other people are also selling hot dogs, Eddy has **COMPETITION.**

Eddy's hot dog stand is called a **FIRM.**

His cost of getting into business is called his **CAPITAL INVESTMENT.**

What Eddy spends to operate his business and create his hot dogs is called **COST.**

The amount that Eddy brings in from the sale of his hot dogs is called **INCOME.**

If Eddy's income is *more* than his cost, the difference is called **PROFIT.** (Eddy really hopes he makes a profit!)

If Eddy's income is *less* than his cost, the difference is called **LOSS.**

If the hot dog business goes really well and Eddy sells lots of hot dogs, it's called a **BOOM**.

If his business activity slows down, it's called a **RECESSION**.

If there is a sustained increase in all prices, including Eddy's hot dogs, that's called **INFLATION**.

If business goes so well that Eddy has to hire someone to help, that's called **LABOR**.

The amount Eddy pays for the help is called **WAGES**.

If Eddy purchases a machine to do the labor instead of a person, that's **AUTOMATION**.

Mechanization and automation can lead to **UNEMPLOYMENT**.

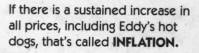

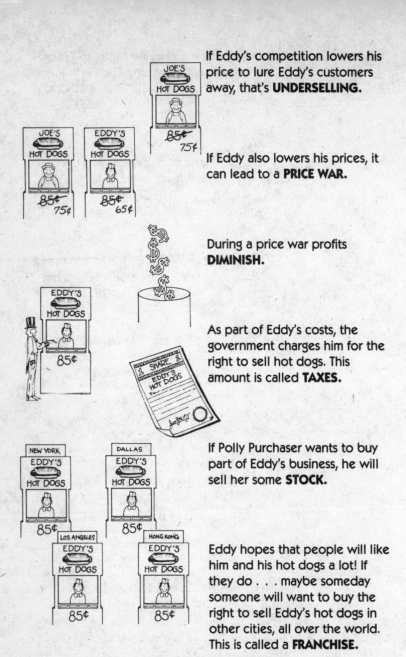

If Eddy's competition lowers his price to lure Eddy's customers away, that's **UNDERSELLING.**

If Eddy also lowers his prices, it can lead to a **PRICE WAR.**

During a price war profits **DIMINISH.**

As part of Eddy's costs, the government charges him for the right to sell hot dogs. This amount is called **TAXES.**

If Polly Purchaser wants to buy part of Eddy's business, he will sell her some **STOCK.**

Eddy hopes that people will like him and his hot dogs a lot! If they do . . . maybe someday someone will want to buy the right to sell Eddy's hot dogs in other cities, all over the world. This is called a **FRANCHISE.**

IV. AREAS OF ECONOMIC CONFUSION

Through personal observation and informal surveys, it seems that confusion about the economy centers mostly around the subjects of money, banking and the Federal Reserve system, and inflation.

A. Money

It is easy to think that you work for money and that money as such, is the object of work. However, in 1758, philosopher David Hume stated,

> Money is not, properly speaking, one of the subjects of commerce, but only the instrument which men have agreed upon to facilitate the exchange of one commodity for another. It is none of the wheels of trade: It is the oil which renders the motions of the wheels more smooth and easy (David Hume, "Of Money," in *Gateway to the Great Books* [Chicago: Encyclopedia Britannica, 1963], 7:92.).

The tragic misconception that money is wealth causes people to do many funny things, such as hold on to modern money as a store of wealth, either by stuffing a mattress or a savings account yielding 5 1/4 percent interest, while inflation is eating it up at the rate of 13 percent. In the history of mankind, money has always tended to shrink rather than stretch with age, and has always ended up being a poor standard for future payment. When money fails to maintain its power to purchase, it fails to remain money.

Even in the Parable of the Talents, Christ was harsh on the steward who *kept* the money for the money's sake by burying it in the ground (Mt. 25:14-20). Money is simply a medium of exchange, *relied upon* largely because of *convenience* and *accepted* because of *confidence*.

Since the silver was extracted even from the Kennedy half dollar in 1964, the coins in your pocket are not intrinsically worth very much. And paper currency in your pocket is worth even less.

Historically, no one person simply sat down and invented money! There has nearly always been some type of money in existence. Early primitive families grouped together in tribes for protection and convenience. Soon there was *division of labor* based on talent and need. They invented stone weapons and crude tools.

Imagine, for instance, ol' "Scarface-Salesman Sam" who was good at making stone clubs for killing animals. Since his accident, ol' "Two-Toes Tom" didn't do too well hunting but could chisel out a great stone plow. "Wanda Wonder-Weaver" couldn't hunt and was too tiny to handle a plow, but could weave a great blanket. "Healthy-Hunter Harold" always had more meat than he could eat.

Adam Smith commented on this type of situation in *The Wealth of Nations* (New York: Modern Library, 1937) . . .

> When the division of labour has once been thoroughly established, it is but a very small part of a man's wants which the product of his own labour can supply. He supplies the far greater part of them by

exchanging that surplus part of the produce of his own labour, which is over and above his own consumption, for such parts of the produce of other men's labour as he has occasion for. Every man thus lives by exchanging, or becomes in some measure a merchant and the society grows to be what is properly a commercial society.

Because he couldn't hunt, Two-Toes Tom became hungry. He had to rely on someone else to provide his meat supply. Maybe Tom could trade for some of Harold's extra meat. But alas . . . the last thing that Healthy-Hunter Harold wanted was one of those crazy stone plows belonging to Two-Toes Tom. However, Healthy-Hunter Harold could use some new stone clubs from Scarface-Salesman Sam. But Sam who hunted occasionally had all the meat he needed. However, he needed a blanket. Certainly a trade could be put together, but it was getting complicated!

There needed to be a more *convenient way*.

Over the years it was observed that nearly everyone in the tribe fancied and collected tiger teeth. Some folks used them as jewelry, some carried them to overcome superstition, and some used them to poke in their ears so they could not hear the little children scream and fuss. The teeth were quite scarce and represented the skill and courage of some tribesmen. They were easily distinguished from rabbit teeth or cow teeth which were not as scarce. Little by little the teeth began to have an agreed-upon value, and they seemed to always be in demand. Scarface-Salesman Sam now felt comfortable in "selling" four stone clubs for 40 tiger teeth, because he knew that he could take the 40 teeth and "purchase" two beautiful blankets from Wanda Wonder-Weaver. Wanda could use some to purchase meat from ol' Healthy-Hunter Harold. Everyone seemed happy, and using the tiger teeth as a medium of exchange certainly was more *convenient*. Throughout history, people have used some very strange things as "money," e.g., salt, hides, wives, tree bark, cattle, wheat, and beads.

A product that is used as "money" usually must possess the following characteristics:
- ease of identification
- durability
- consistency of quality
- portability
- divisibility without loss of other basic characteristics
- relative stability of supply
- usefulness for something other than money.

In early America there was a real shortage of coins or currency. For that reason Peter Minuit in 1626 purchased Manhattan Island from the Indians for approximately $25.00 worth of seashells and colored beads. Later, the main medium of exchange in America became tobacco. However, down through the ages the most acceptable commodity to be used as money has been metal.

Shoppers used to carry bars of metal to the ancient markets to make their purchases. Whatever quantity of silver or gold was required as the purchase price would be cut from the bar, weighed very carefully, and given to the merchant. The merchant would collect many of these chips and melt them again into bars. Later, for reasons of *convenience*, this practice gave way to the minting of coins which were easily identifiable, had their weight and purity stamped on them, and usually bore the image and guarantee of some governmental leader. The convenience of the usage of "coins" was attained at the expense of *government regulation and control*. For sooner or later governments have *always* taken over the control of *seigniorage*, i.e., the sovereign right to mint coins and print currency. Paper money is also printed for reasons of convenience, with the basic understanding that it is backed by an equivalent amount of gold, silver, etc., and may be exchanged for such at any time. The first paper money in America came not from banks but from the governments in the colonies. In 1690 Massachusetts issued paper money, but it had nothing to back it except promises of redemption. This privilege was soon abused, and the market was flooded with paper money. This drove the coins out of circulation (they were hoarded because they had *real value*) and caused prices to soar. By 1751 Britain demanded that no more paper money could be issued.

The Mint Act of 1792, which has survived almost intact until the present, adopted the dollar as the standard unit of currency and the decimal system of counting.

Without doubt, many of the ancients would have blinked their eyes and scratched their heads in disbelief at the incredible feat accomplished by modern governments to persuade the electorates to accept *paper* as money. Their question would be, "What gives paper any purchasing power?" For a time the answer might have been that all paper money in the United States was backed by its equivalent of gold stored in Fort Knox, Ky., and anytime you wanted to trade your "greenback" for gold, you could do so.

However, in 1933 the United States abandoned the national gold standard and has never since returned. Today the nation's gold reserves amount to only a fraction of the nation's money supply. For example, on January 1, 1987, the nation's M2 money supply including currency, demand deposits, time deposits, and money market funds totaled $2,800 billion. At the same time, the value of gold owned by the government amounted to only $11.15 billion. Each dollar, therefore, was backed by less than 1/2 cent of gold.

The only reason paper money has purchasing power today is because people *accept* it as having value. You accept paper money in payment because you have *confidence* in the fact that other people will accept your paper money when you wish to purchase something. Thus, it is *confidence* that becomes the basis for *value*. If for some reason a certain percentage of people decided that they would no longer accept paper money as payment, it quickly would go out of circulation. However, it would have to be *replaced by something else*, since it would be difficult to even imagine a modern economy functioning without some form of money.

One form of "money" which has emerged into existence in your lifetime is the plastic credit card. Credit cards are issued by an institution to a holder to be used as a form of money. Credit cards are not considered in the truest sense "money," in that it requires another form of money to satisfy payment for the statement received at the end of the month. However, more and more the trend is to consider the credit card usage as direct authorization of transfer of value from the institution to the merchant.

Recently there have been many authors who have admonished their readers to perform "plastic surgery" and cut up all credit cards. This perhaps is a normal response where there is not the basic understanding of the concept of money. However, it is simply a medium for exchange to conveniently facilitate the trading of the excess of your labor in one area for the excess of someone else's labor specialty. The problem with credit cards lies not with the medium of exchange but with the discipline involved in utilizing that medium of exchange.

Many credit card holders, because of the printout of monthly transactions, have a better system of bookkeeping than they ever did when paying cash and having no record of the transaction. The abuse of the credit card and its privileges is short range at the most. You might say, "computer money is a TERMINAL ILLNESS." As with the use of any other medium of exchange, either you abide by the card rules or you are quickly out of the *card game*. You will not have the privilege of remaining undisciplined very long.

It has been very interesting to observe the changes in recent history as the people of the United States move farther and farther away from the Great Depression of the 1930s. There has been a gradual transition from the demand for using only hard coin and currency to the use of time deposits, demand deposits, checking accounts, NOW accounts (Negotiable Order of Withdrawal), and credit cards. At this time it is estimated that of our *present* U.S. monetary system, only five percent is in coin or currency and 95 percent is in banking "paper transactions."

Remember, *money is simply a medium of exchange relied upon largely because of convenience and accepted because of confidence.* Maybe what you know as money will buy wealth for you; maybe it will not. This concept must be understood before you can expect to understand how the Federal Reserve system changes the national debt into new money and before you can fully appreciate how inflation takes wealth from you like a thief in the night.

B. The Federal Reserve System

Another economic phenomenon which seems to be a mystery to most is the business of banking. Relatively few people seem to understand how much their lives are affected by this awesome industry. To gain an insight into the modern banking system, you must first take a look back into history.

When "Barney Businessman" was fortunate enough to accumulate a sizeable amount of gold or silver as a result of his business dealings, he was then confronted with the problem of keeping it safe from those who would forcibly redistribute it: *thieves and robbers.*

Because "Gaffney Goldsmith's" business was that of dealing in precious metals, he had been forced to construct a thief-proof vault. It was only natural then that Barney Businessman would go to Gaffney and request of him space in his vault to store his accumulated gold. In fact, Barney was willing to pay Gaffney a fee for the "safekeeping" of his gold. Of course, when Barney deposited his gold into Gaffney's vault, he requested and received a *receipt of deposit* which he had to present whenever he wished to reclaim his gold. Other people in the community began to realize that Gaffney Goldsmith's vault was an extremely safe and convenient place to keep their gold. In fact, Gaffney's vault became somewhat of a warehouse for gold.

Gaffney was quite intelligent, and it didn't take him long to realize that on any given day, 80 to 90 percent of the gold in his vault simply sat there collecting dust. There was never a day when everyone came to his vault and wanted their gold . . . all at the same time. Any daily withdrawals of gold were offset by that day's receipts of gold. And since gold is gold, no one seemed to care whose gold he received when he wanted to make a withdrawal. Therefore, Gaffney usually made all of his transactions out of the few bags of gold in the front of his vault while all the bags in the back sat there collecting dust and taking up a lot of valuable vault space. Gaffney realized that he had a good thing going . . . and his books always balanced!

One day "Fenwick Farmer," who had tried desperately, but unsuccessfully, to borrow some money from his family, happened by Gaffney Goldsmith's place. He was wanting to borrow some money to make some purchases for the farm that would *increase his earning ability* and *raise his standard of living.*

Fenwick asked Gaffney if it would be possible to borrow some of the dust-covered gold from the back of his vault. He said he would even be willing to pay rent on the gold while he was using it. This was of *interest.* Gaffney, wanting to be honest and forthright, and always wanting his books to balance, went to Barney Businessman, who owned some of the dust-covered gold in the back of the vault. He explained to Barney that Fenwick Farmer was willing to pay a fee for the temporary usage of the gold and return the original sum out of the increased proceeds from the farm which would be made possible from the new purchases. The deal was made upon Fenwick signing a *promissory note to repay* and upon Gaffney's agreeing to split the "*interest money*" equally with Barney. Gaffney also assured Barney that if he needed some gold before Fenwick repaid his loan, he was sure he could talk one of the other depositors into lending Barney some of their unused gold on the same kind of basis. Everyone was happy! And Gaffney's books still balanced.

GAFFNEY GOLDSMITH

Assets		Liabilities & Net Worth	
Gold	$1,500	Receipts	$2,000
Note	500		
	$2,000		

(Note: The total assets remain unchanged; only the form is changed.)

Based upon Gaffney's experience that taught him that there never was a time when *all* the people wanted *all* of their gold withdrawn *at one time,* he began feeling comfortable in lending out more and more of his reserve. Since he was making money from lending out the gold, he soon began enticing depositors to place gold in his vault by paying *them,* rather than them paying him for storage and *safe*keeping. This was the forerunner of our modern concept of *fractional reserve banking.* All Gaffney had to do was to keep enough gold supply on hand to take care of each day's transactions.

64

An additional step which the ancient goldsmiths discovered brought us closer to the banking system that we know today.

Fenwick made a discovery. He had signed a promissory note and had borrowed the gold from Gaffney Goldsmith, yet *he* also needed a safe place to keep his gold until he actually purchased his farm improvements. Obviously, the safest place to keep his gold was in the vault of Gaffney Goldsmith. Gaffney agreed to keep Fenwick's gold in his vault and gave Fenwick a *deposit receipt* for his gold. Gaffney had no problem with this transaction because his books still balanced.

GAFFNEY GOLDSMITH

Assets		Liabilities & Net Worth	
Gold	$2,000	Receipts to depositors	$2,000
Note	500	Receipts to borrower	500
	$2,500		$2,500

But even though Gaffney's books balanced, the fact that his totals increased caused him to be curious as to the effect the Fenwick transaction would have on the total economy of the village.

One of the purchases that Fenwick intended to make was that of a new, larger farm wagon to haul his produce to market. He paid a visit to the shop of "Wiseman Wagonright," who built the finest wagons that ever rolled on four wooden wheels. Fenwick found just the right wagon and agreed to make the purchase. He explained to Wiseman that he would need to go clear over to the other side of the village to draw out enough gold from Gaffney's vault to pay him. But Wiseman, who portrayed the very characteristics of his name, thought that to be quite a waste of time and effort. He explained to Fenwick that he kept all of his gold in Gaffney's vault as well, and there was certainly no need for Fenwick to go withdraw the gold and deliver it to Wiseman for the wagon. This, he explained, would only cause Wiseman to make another special trip over to Gaffney's to deposit the same gold back into the vault yet that same day. What a waste of effort! Wiseman then suggested that Fenwick either give him part of his gold deposit receipt from Gaffney or write an authorization note for Gaffney to transfer gold from Fenwick's account to the account Wiseman Wagonright. Thus the origin of our modern checking accounts. (Discoveries have been made of clay slabs from ancient Babylon as well as ancient goldsmiths' receipts which were used in "checking accounts" of the past.)

As Gaffney Goldsmith completed this transaction and entered it into his books, he realized the real impact of the increased totals on his books:

> *If the receipts to borrowers are used as money, then the goldsmith actually created money by making loans and issuing those receipts.*

Each loan issued increased the money supply and the purchasing power in circulation, even though the supply of gold had not changed at all!

You have now been able to observe how the ancient goldsmiths were essentially performing the same activities as the modern bank where you do your business:
1. Taking in deposits
2. Making loans
3. Issuing and honoring deposit receipts that in effect become money.

No doubt you have already asked yourself the question: "What would keep the lending institution from lending out more money by issuing notes than there was real money in the vault? Then how would I get my money back?"

In order to answer that question, you must examine again the element of confidence. As long as you are *convinced* that you *could* go to the bank and withdraw all of your deposits at any given time, then you would be equally *convinced* that it would be foolish to *actually do it and lose your interest for that time.*

Your agreement with your bank when you make a deposit is that they will return your money to you whenever you demand it if it is in a checking account or within a period of a few months if it is in some form of a savings account. This is a promise that the banker only *presumes* he can keep. Your money is then taken, and the majority of it is loaned to someone who may not be required to repay the money for perhaps 20 or 30 years. Obviously, the bank cannot technically keep both agreements. However, history has proven that if the element of *confidence* is present, new depositors will put more money into the bank and, out of that new deposit, you can receive your money if you so demand.

In the late 1700s the young government of the United States quickly realized the need for some type of control over banking. However, independence and freedom were the key items in the development of early America, and the fear of federal control and "money monopoly" frustrated any successful attempt by the government to bridle banking. "Wildcat banking" was prevalent, and since all banks were scrambling to make a profit, many banks failed due to undisciplined management. The bank panics of 1819, 1837, and 1857 brought about the National Banking Act of 1864. In 1900 the United States went on the *gold standard* which was to stabilize the economy by making all forms of U.S. currency redeemable with gold. But following the panic of 1907, congress was persuaded that the reason for all the country's economic "ups and downs" was that there was no *central banking system.* They claimed that with such a system there would be control over the nation's total money supply and the central bank could step in and protect the depositors of any bank that had become over extended. It was argued that this would guarantee once and for all the *confidence* in the banking system.

Thus, two days before Christmas, 1913, President Woodrow Wilson signed the Federal Reserve Act. There was *strong reluctance* on the part of the individual banks to create a strong central system in Washington, D.C., or New York, so the Federal Reserve Act became somewhat of a compromise. It divided the country into 12 districts with each district containing a Federal Reserve bank and additional branch banks. All banks with "National Bank" designation were required to join, but the state banks only joined if they so desired.

The Federal Reserve bank is a separate organization, not under the direct control of congress or the president of the United States. However, the president does appoint any vacancy on the Board of Governors. The Board of Governors, which consists of seven members, each appointed for a 14-year term, completely supervises the Federal Reserve system.

You could not walk into a Federal Reserve bank and make a deposit or negotiate a loan. A Federal Reserve bank is a "banker's bank" which receives deposits, holds reserves, issues notes and currency, and clears checks . . . just for banks. However, you are affected by an agency known as the Federal Depositors Insurance Corporation (FDIC) which also serves to bolster your *confidence* in the Federal Reserve system by claiming that every bank account is guaranteed up to $100,000. This tends to increase your *confidence* and alleviate your fears of making deposits in your local bank, even though you subconsciously know that the institution could ultimately cover only slightly over one penny for every dollar on deposit.

The U.S. Treasury prints paper money and mints coins, but the Federal Reserve system alone is authorized to place them into circulation. The U.S. Treasury also maintains its deposits from taxations, fees, etc., in the "Fed," which it is often called.

The Board of Governors is assisted by a Federal Advisory Council and the Federal Open Market Committee which is in charge of buying and selling government securities. (We will see the importance of this committee later, and its role in inflation.) Of course, the old, established banks had no desire to be controlled. But they had lobbied congress for government regulations to make it more difficult for additional banks to enter into the competition and to keep the other established banks from initiating competitive practices which would have affected their profits. Perhaps it was due to these ulterior motives that the Federal Reserve system failed so miserably in helping to ward off the Great Depression and the bank crashes of 1929.

A most important fact to remember is that the Federal Reserve Board has ultimate control over *the money supply* of the United States. They have the power to either increase or decrease the total amount of money in the monetary system. The Federal Reserve Board utilizes three basic methods in its alteration of the money supply.

1. Through its control of the fractional reserve requirements.

The fractional reserve requirement is the control that would have kept our imaginary Gaffney Goldsmith from loaning out too much of his gold. Each lending institution is required to maintain a certain percentage of its deposits in reserve, either in their own vaults or on deposit in one of the Federal Reserve banks. The Fed has the right to raise or lower the percentage of those reserves within congressional limits. Quite simply, if the Fed requires the bank to retain a larger percentage of the deposits, then there is less money to be loaned out, thus the money supply tends to fall. If the reserve requirement is lowered, then the money supply tends to expand, and it is easier for you to borrow the bank's money.

2. Through its control of the discount rate.

Banks not only use their customers' money but they also borrow money from the Fed. The rate at which banks borrow money from the Federal Reserve is known as the *discount rate.* As the discount rate is *lowered*, it becomes more attractive for the banks to borrow. The banks borrow so that they can loan more money out to their customers. When money is loaned out to borrowers, the money supply expands. When the *discount rate* is *increased* by the Fed, there is a tendency for the banks to borrow less. Therefore, there is a tendency for the banks to loan out less to their customers, and the money supply tends to shrink.

The "prime rate" is the rate of interest charged by a bank to its best customers. *Prime rate* is largely determined by the Fed's discount rate and the customers' demand for money. If the prime rate gets too high, it becomes impractical for the customers to borrow.

3. *Through its activities of buying or selling notes and securities of the*
   U.S. Treasury.

This procedure will be explained in more detail in the next section. But let it be simply stated here that the most dramatic method for altering the money supply is through the "monetizing" of the *Government's deficit spending* by the Federal Reserve system.

It has been important for you to take the time to understand the concept of "money" and to learn the functions of the "Banking System." Without this knowledge it would be difficult for you to understand the origin and effect of perhaps the most serious threat to any economy . . . *inflation.*

C. Inflation

Inflation is an economic phenomenon where a sustained increase takes place in *all* prices. It is a result of overspending and overborrowing and necessitates the government's creating additional money and placing that newly created money in the economic system. Inflation takes place when you want more things than you can afford, so you simply make more money out of thin air in order to make those purchases.

In the Fall of 1983 the Federal Reserve bank published its research findings regarding the recent behavior of inflation. Its conclusion only reaffirmed the already known fact that "a one percentage point increase in the long-run average growth of money will lead to an increase in inflation of about one percentage point. That is, there is a one-to-one correspondence between money growth and inflation over the long-run, and non-monitary factors may account for significant departures from that rate over shorter time periods. It is premature to conclude that runaway inflation is now safely behind us" (Federal Reserve Bank, REVIEW, R.W. Hafer, August/September, 1983, Vol. 65, No. 7, p. 39).

Regardless of what you have heard through the media, inflation is not dead. And for that reason let's investigate some of the history and characteristics of inflation and how it affects your life-style.

During the 1930s this country experienced an extremely painful phenomenon called a depression. The depression followed several years of high-flying speculation and risky leverage investing during the "roaring '20s." But the rising burden of debt service charges and the growing reality that borrowers were being forced to sell their new investments to try to cover even a small percentage of their gigantic debts caused a panic. In 1929 that panic spread to the banks. The banks had made loans far in excess of their liquid assets. When the borrowers were unable to repay their debts the banks were forced to close. The bank depositors were left with nothing since the banks had given credit and loaned out money that in reality didn't exist.

When the balloon burst and the dust settled it became evident that the real money supply was only a fraction of what it had artificially been publicized to be.

The rapid contraction of the money supply left the entire economy depressed. No longer was there money available for new business ventures. The short supply of money restricted purchases. Unemployment was rampant because there was no money to pay wages. Without the grease of a money supply, the wheels of commerce screeched nearly to a halt.

The panic caused congress to enact economic protectionist measures like the Smoot-Hawley Tariff. Those efforts were designed to keep what money there was left from being spent on imports. A catastrophic trade and currency war ensued and the rest of the world descended with us into the Great Depression.

President Roosevelt responded with a policy based on the suggestion of the English economist John Maynard Keynes. The President implemented a plan to replenish the grease for the economic wheels. He began creating new money . . . from out of thin air. But with the newly created money he began government programs that put the people back to work. The workers spent the money on local purchases. The government began spending large sums of money on national projects, and the money supply began to expand. However, it was not until the U.S. Government began creating and spending billions of dollars to finance World War II that the depression actually ended.

An interesting by-product came about as a result of the depression episode. The American people, politicians and constituents alike, adopted a mind-set of spending their way out of economic troubles. That mind-set has resulted over the years in behavioral excess. When it has appeared that the economy was showing signs of another money supply contraction or business recession the government has been quick to "fine tune" the economy by creating new money again and pumping it into the lagging economy. For certainly, no one ever wanted another depression!

To some extent, this "fine tuning" was kept in check for a while by the United States tying its money supply to a gold standard where money could only be created to an equal amount of our gold supply. Following World War II the Bretton Woods agreement established an international standard based on gold, and the strength of the United States dollar.

However, Richard Nixon violated that agreement in 1971 and severed the link between the international gold standard and the supply of money. With the checks and balances now removed the creating and spending mind-set of the American people went into high gear, and has been setting economic speed records to this day.

But, during the 1980s the Reagan administration made it appear that inflation was eliminated even though the spending and borrowing increased. That illusion was accomplished by several factors. *First,* the price of energy went down. The oil cartels had produced a glut of oil and faced real competition with each other for sales. *Second,* the interest rates were kept high on the United States Government securities which attracted large amounts of foreign money into our system. We were paying for our spending habits with other countries' money.

The strong dollar allowed us to purchase large quantities of cheap imported goods, like shoes from Brazil, clothes from Korea, tools from India, etc. The importing of cheap goods made it appear that our overall prices were not increasing.

But the strong dollar had an adverse effect on our exports. Foreign countries could not afford to purchase our goods. In essence, we swapped the effects of inflation for historically high trade deficits on the short range and continued to overspend and overborrow and create new money at record levels. In order to correct the situation, another depression will occur or another round of undisguised inflation will be experienced. No one wants to go through another depression, so, it is most likely that inflation will again take off. The latter alternative is especially appealing since it can be done without anyone really assuming the blame.

Inflation is nothing new. Of all the numerous currencies created throughout the world since the 1700s, very few of them still exist in their original form. America's Continental dollar was first issued in 1775. By 1779 the amount in circulation had increased from $6 million to $242 million. By 1781 it took 225 Continentals to buy one dollar in specie coin, and final quotations ranged from 500-1,000 to one. In 1789 Alexander Hamilton finally redeemed 100 old Continental dollars for one new "hard" dollar. No doubt you are aware of what happened to the German reichsmark following World War I when people would pay as high as 750,000 marks for some simple groceries . . . if they could find any for sale; also stories of how they would take a wheelbarrow full of money to the store only to have someone on the way dump out the worthless money and steal the wheelbarrow. By 1922-23 there were four quintillion marks in existence. All of the savings and financial assets of the German people were wiped out. They had to start over.

Since World War II, Argentina, Bolivia, Chile, and Uruguay all have had to reform their currency systems because of runaway inflation. Brazil called in 1,000 old cruzeiros for the new one. Greece has had to exchange 1,000 old drachmas for one new. France had a 100 to one franc exchange due to their inflation problems.

But before we continue our discussion, let's recall that inflation is a sustained increase in the general level of all prices.

In the United States, inflation is most commonly measured by the Consumer Price Index (CPI) constructed by the U.S. Department of Labor, Bureau of Labor Statistics. The Bureau determines the sustained increase in the general level of all prices by measuring the percent change in the cost of a "bundle" or "market basket" of selected goods and services from one year to another or from one period of time to another. The "bundle" includes several thousand items sold by about 23,000 establishments in 85 cities. The CPI is often referred to as the *average inflation rate*. Following you will find the annual inflation rates for the United States including the years 1930-86.

U.S. annual inflation rates, five-year averages, 1930-86

Period	Average inflation rate	Period	Average inflation rate
1930-34	-4.7%	1975-78	7.3%
1935-39	0.8%	1979	11.3%
1940-44	4.9%	1980	13.5%
1945-49	6.4%	1981	10.4%
1950-54	2.5%	1982	6.1%
1955-59	1.6%	1983	3.2%
1960-64	1.2%	1984	4.3%
1965-69	3.4%	1985	3.6%
1970-74	6.1%	1986	1.9%

As you can see, inflation has made unparalleled increases since 1969 . . . which brings us back to the question of who or what causes inflation?

FRANK AND ERNEST by Bob Thaves

COUNCIL OF ECONOMIC ADVISERS

IF WE CAN'T SLOW INFLATION DOWN, WHY DON'T WE JUST SPEED EVERYTHING ELSE UP?

THAVES 10-22

Reprinted by permission. © 1981 NEA, Inc.

The fact is, *inflation is not caused by individual producers raising their prices.* This is true whether you are talking about oil cartels, individual merchants, labor unions, or certain industries. Remember, inflation is a sustained increase in the general level of all prices. But if only *one price goes up, then the other price must come down.* For instance if an oil cartel, such as OPEC, raises its price of oil by $12 billion, there should be $12 billion less in the system for consumers to purchase other goods. These other goods would then sit on the shelves and go unpurchased or their price would come down, thus causing a *recession* in business. The raising of individual prices through scarcity, monopolies, wage and price fights, etc., does not *cause* inflation, i.e., a sustained increase in the general level of *all* prices. You will see a little later that the raising of prices is a necessary *result* of inflation, not the cause.

It is *when the money supply is increased* while the supply of goods stays the same that you cut the purchasing power of the money. That is, it takes more money to purchase the same product, in fact more money to purchase all products. Then we have "a sustained increase in general level of all prices" or *inflation.*

Another way to state it is to say that when there is a sustained increase in the general level of all prices, it is because there has been a sustained *decrease* in the general *value of the money.*

No doubt by now you can see why it was of such importance for you to understand the concept of "money" as was discussed in a previous section. An *increase* in the supply of money relative to the supply of goods is the *cause of inflation.* Without the possibility of the sovereign government being able to alter the supply of money in the system, there would be no inflation. But how do modern governments actually go about increasing the money supply?

Consider now two contemporary methods used to alter the money supply: (1) through use of the Fractional Reserve System, and (2) through monetizing of the Federal Deficit.

THE WIZARD OF ID   by Brant parker and Johnny hart

EXTRA, EXTRA... KING SAYS PRICES WILL DROP

I'LL TAKE ONE, SONNY

THAT WILL BE TWENTY-FIVE CENTS

HERE'S A DIME

THE LITTLE NIPPER SHOULD READ THE PAPERS

By permission of Johnny Hart and Field Enterprises, Inc.

1. THE FRACTIONAL RESERVE SYSTEM

As you will recall from our previous discussion about the Federal

Reserve system, each depository institution is required to *maintain a certain percentage of its deposits in reserve* . . . either in its own vaults or on deposit in one of the Federal Reserve banks. The reserve requirements may vary from three percent to 16 1/4 percent, depending upon the size of the institution. Many people assume that the legal reserve requirements were set up to protect depositors. Other people argue that the action was initiated to protect the bankers from the public; i.e., the people would feel like they were being protected by the government, thereupon the banks could expand their deposits and loans without the danger of bank runs. Perhaps an equally valid reason for maintaining legal reserve requirements is to give a means of control to the Federal Reserve Board over the maximum amount of bank loans, thereby governing to some degree the *quantity of money in the economy.*

Remember when Gaffney Goldsmith made a loan to Fenwick Farmer and Fenwick left the gold in Gaffney's vault, taking instead a deposit receipt? Fenwick discovered that he could use the deposit receipt as "money" and still leave all the gold in the vault for safekeeping. You will also recall that the transaction astounded Gaffney, because he realized that by so doing he had suddenly created more money in the system:

(Before Fenwick's Loan)
GAFFNEY GOLDSMITH

Assets		Liabilities & Net Worth	
Gold	$2,000	Receipts to Depositors	$2,000

(After Fenwick's Loan)
GAFFNEY GOLDSMITH

Assets		Liabilities & Net Worth	
Gold	$2,000	Receipts to Depositors	$2,000
Note	500		
	$2,500	Receipts to Borrower	500
			$2,500

Even though today's modern banking practices are a little more sophisticated, the principles work exactly the same. Every time a bank makes a loan, the money supply is expanded.

Let's say that "Billy Banker" has a bank that falls under today's five percent reserve category. That means that out of every $100 deposited in Billy's bank, he has to keep $5.00 in reserve.

Let's say Billy Banker has $10,000 in his bank. The checks coming in to Billy's bank have offset checks going out. So his balance sheet shows $10,000 in demand deposit liabilities and $10,000 in total reserves. The five percent requirement demands that Billy keep $500 in reserve either in his vault or the vault at the Federal Reserve bank. The remaining 95 percent, i.e., the $9,500 *excess reserve, is the amount that can be loaned out to the public.* Billy is eager to get this amount loaned out, because the interest return on money loaned out is his prime source of income for his bank.

The next morning Carlton Contractor walks into the bank wanting a $9,500 loan to build a new garage. He has no problem with the interest rate or duration of the loan, so he signs a promissory note. Billy sets up a checking account for Carlton and deposits the proceeds of the loan into the account. When that check is *deposited* into Billy's bank, $9,500 of new money has just been created. The five percent reserve requirement demands that $475 of Carlton's money actually remain in reserve, bringing the total required reserve to $975. However, please note that Billy still has $9,025 in *excess reserves* to be loaned out again to the public. This expansion of the money supply takes place regardless of whether the funds stay in one bank or are processed through many banks. You can see that if Billy Banker loans out the $9,025 now in excess reserves, the amount which started out as $10,000 will have now grown to $28,525 in two simple steps. Surely this would startle even Gaffney Goldsmith!

As you might suspect, this new money in the system "heats up" the economy and gives the illusion of a business boom and allows the consumption of many goods and products at the old price level. But because of the injection of the new money, these goods and products will have to be replaced by higher-priced items.

Regulating the *fractional reserve requirements* and *discount rates* are methods used by the Fed to keep this explosive expansion under control. Remember: an increase in the supply of "money" relative to the supply of goods is the cause of inflation.

2. MONETIZING OF THE FEDERAL DEFICIT

As volatile as the Fractional Reserve System's method of expanding the money supply through bank loans might appear, it doesn't hold a candle to the operation of monetizing the national debt. The U.S. Treasury Department keeps most of its money in the Federal Reserve bank. Checks are written on this account for every government expenditure. However, upon occasion, those in the federal government have an interesting problem: they spend more than they have in their account. Perhaps this has happened to you before, but I'll bet you've never overdrawn your account by trillions of dollars!

If you were overdrawn, you basically had two ways of covering the deficit. Either you hurried around and earned enough to cover the amount, or you found someone who would make you a quick loan. The federal government does not earn money, so it is left with the choice of either quickly levying a new tax to raise the money, or . . . going to the marketplace to get a loan.

But, think for a moment: Who could loan the government trillions of dollars just to cover the extravagant spending habits of congress? Lots of people—together that is! The government does not simply go to one source and borrow the money. They make thousands and thousands of little loans in the form of U.S. Treasury bills (T-bills), notes, and security bonds. They are essentially government I.O.U.'s given in return for the borrowed money. These securities are auctioned off. The Treasury Department encourages these loans by offering high rates of interest. The I.O.U.'s (T-bills, notes, and bonds) are purchased through dealers by individuals, pension funds, public corporations, insurance companies, trust funds, and sometimes by foreign countries wishing to invest in the security of the United Sates. However, many of the securities are purchased by *banks*. This would make good common sense. As you will recall, banks are required to retain a percentage of their deposits as "required reserves" . . . to be kept in their own vaults or in the vaults of their regional Federal Reserve bank. But if the money is just held in the vaults, the banks will receive *no interest*. But if they exchange their required reserves for government T-bills or bonds, they will receive a high rate of interest. And, of course, the Federal Reserve Board would approve of this: "It's good for everybody."

Many less sophisticated countries simply print paper money to pay for the cost overruns of their governments, finding that form of taxation to be a simpler method than the one used by the United States. But, you will recall, *increasing the supply of money in the system causes inflation.* And so far, our illustration has not injected new money into the system. It would be as if there were ten dollars and ten cherry pies in the system. The government wanted one of the cherry pies but did not have a dollar to pay for it. So it would offer a bond, presuming that there would be one person in the system who would rather have an interest-bearing bond than a cherry pie. So now you have ten dollars, ten cherry pies, and one bond in the system.

However, continuing to pay high interest on the old debt doesn't really make sense . . . especially when it amounts to over $100 billion each year! So it would only seem reasonable for the Federal

Reserve bank to step in and change that debt from interest-bearing debt (T-bills and bonds) to noninterest-bearing debt, paid for by a type of taxation, i.e., inflation. The Federal Open Market Committee of the Federal Reserve bank begins to call in those T-bills and bonds and pay them off. What do they use to pay off these securities? You guessed it . . . *newly created money!*

This process is accomplished by the Federal Reserve bank issuing a check to the bond dealer who in turn deposits that check into his bank account. The check, when it is deposited, is credited by the Federal Reserve bank to that bank's reserves, and that bank is then entitled to make loans against that new reserve or exchange it for cash. Why did the Federal Reserve bank have the right to issue the check? Because it was backed up by the U.S. Treasury I.O.U. that it just purchased!

THE WIZARD OF ID   by Brant Parker and Johnny Hart

By permission of Johnny Hart and Field Enterprises, Inc.

In essence, what has happened in this transaction is that the federal debt—*a liability*—has been transformed *into an asset* by the U.S. Treasury's signing of a note. The note is an asset of the Federal Reserve bank. In other words, the *debt of the government* has been miraculously turned into spendable money.

That is called . . . monetizing the federal deficit.

The basic U.S. money supply was growing at a 20.2 percent annual rate from April, 1986, through December, 1986, one of the fastest rates in history. The total current national debt as of January, 1987, was over $2 1/4 trillion ($2,225,000,000,000.00). The debt had doubled between January, 1983, and December, 1986.

Monetizing the national debt by using the intermediate step of issuing bonds, stalls the impact on the economy for a year or more. But it has *exactly the same ultimate effect* as if the government did not issue the bonds in the first place, but simply paid its debt with printing-press money. Instead of having ten dollars and ten cherry pies and one bond in the system, there would now be 11 dollars, ten cherry pies, and no bond. the outcome is that there is new money injected into the monetary supply which lowers the value of the rest of the money and causes a sustained increase in the general level of *all* prices, i.e., *inflation.*

Remember, inflation is the ultimate, subtle taxation. No one escapes the effects of inflation, there is no cost to the government for collecting tax, and the government is the sole beneficiary.

There is a distinct advantage to this type of taxation. Congress does not have to accept the responsibility of openly voting to increase taxes on the electorate. They only have to agree to spending more money, which appeals to them since that money can be utilized through projects for their constituents to help return them to congress. This gives the illusion that government has all the answers and an unending supply of money. Congress simply has to approve a deficit-spending budget which will be "monetized" by the U.S. Treasury and Federal Reserve bank into new available money.

How long will inflation continue?

You can answer that question quite simply now that you have discovered that increasing the money supply to cover the government deficit spending is the real cause of inflation. Inflation will stop . . .

1. When deficit spending is discontinued.
2. When all of the present deficit has been monetized.

When dealing with the question of the future of inflation, it is important to remember that inflation is directly related to the *philosophy* toward deficit spending, the *size* of the deficit, and the *rate* at which that deficit is monetized.

Well over half of the deficit is still being held by individuals, companies, pension plans, insurance companies, and banks, in the forms of Treasury bills and bonds. It has not yet been monetized. Therefore, the postponed effect of that balance has yet to be experienced by the economy, to say nothing of the current deficits that are accumulating.

Why does inflation continue?

The other day a lady was overheard admitting, "You know . . . I believe I rather enjoy inflation. It allows me to live in a more expensive neighborhood . . . without moving."

It is true that one of the reasons for the persistence of inflation is that *many people don't want to see it go away.* Based on this, inflation has become self-perpetuating. It was observed earlier how the politician is able to implement programs and projects through deficit spending that allow him to appease special interest groups and local constituents, thereby promoting his own reelection. Without the phenomenon of inflation, much of this would, of necessity, come to a halt. But the politician is not to be held totally responsible at this point, *for the electorate will always find someone who will represent and deliver their desires.*

One of the arguments voiced by founding fathers of our country when trying to decide whether the government should be a true democracy or a true republic, favored the republic concept since they proposed that democracy would only exist until the electorate discovered that by their *voice* in elections, they could *vote monies from the Treasury into their own pockets.* Based on an exaggerated view of the economic philosophy of John Maynard Keynes, who believed that economic security could be attained through increased government spending, this country has produced a generation of people who have sincerely come to believe that the government is a source of wealth. The electorate is only now beginning to see that the money to fund this insatiable spending appetite must come from the people themselves. It must be generated through taxation, and to the present most have failed to see that inflation is nothing more than sophisticated taxation without representation.

Quite obviously, it is going to be extremely difficult for the government to initiate the necessary discipline and self-restraint needed to reverse this vicious cycle of deficit spending, taxation, and inflation. But a cure must be found. Even John Maynard Keynes, in *The Economic Consequences of the Peace* (New York: Harcourt Brace Jovanovich, 1920), understood that:

> There is no sublter, no surer means of overturning the existing basis of society than to debauch the currency. The process engages all the hidden forces of economic law on the side of destruction, and does it in a manner which not one man in a million is able to diagnose (p. 236).

The right to engage in deficit spending, and the right to eliminate that deficit through monetizing the debt, has become an inflationary *addiction.* It seemed so harmless at the start. The increased quantity of money enabled the government to spend more without anybody else having to spend less. Even today many believe that it is only a temporary problem brought on by strange circumstances, and that it will just go away tomorrow on it own accord. But that will never happen. For the addiction, there must be a cure.

During the process of addiction, the good effects come first; . . . the bad effects come later. In the cure, the bad effects come first; . . . the good effects come later.

And in the meantime, there is the almost irresistible urge to shortcut and go for the "cheap kick."

One of the bad effects of the cure is the fact that, classically, when inflation rates go down, *unemployment rates* go up. That is because there is less money available for marginal businesses and jobs. Unemployment is unpopular, therefore shunned by politicians.

Historically, inflation that has been allowed to accelerate, unchecked, sooner or later has so weakened the very fabric of society that the electorate is then compelled to seek change. Following World War I, the hyperinflation in Russia and Germany, which saw prices double or more than double from one day to the next, really prepared the ground for the political experiments of Communism in the one country and Nazism in the other. It was the yielding to the temptation of inflation in China after World War II that eased Chairman Mao's defeat of Chiang Kaishek. In 1954 the Brazilian military government took over when inflation reached 100 percent a year. Likewise, Allende of Chile (1973) and Isabel Peron of Argentina (1976) were overthrown by the military following periods of extreme inflation. It appears that when the electorate finally reaches their limit of exorbitant taxation and inflation, they simply look for some outspoken leader who displays a sense of direction and confidence upon whom they can gratefully thrust the robes of leadership.

Admittedly, the economic situation that you have inherited does not look altogether rosy. And historically, the odds seem to be against a government that tries to come back to its abandoned ideal once it has traveled its distance down the road of greed and nonrestraint. *However*, while directly facing the reality of today, I choose to keep my eyes open to the *opportunities* of tomorrow, realizing that glory can be brought to God in the midst of either economic chaos, or economic grandeur.

5

Solomon's Success Model

Recently I compiled a list of characteristics possessed by those considered successful. After refining my list, I decided to seek the counsel of the wisest man who ever lived: Solomon. What do you think he would have to say about common denominators of success? You can be assured that the advice is trustworthy when it is coming from a person who had lived out the extremely successful years of his life, had come to the end of the road, looked backward over his entire journey, and, in a final statement of summation, simply suggested,

> Here is my final conclusion: fear God and obey his commandments, for this is the entire duty of man. For God will judge us for everything we do, including every hidden thing, good or bad (Eccl. 12:13, TLB).

But let's discover what specific advice Solomon has to share with us today. In fact, let's call our list Solomon's Success Model. And to help us remember the characteristics, let's use the word MODEL as an acrostic.

M—Motivation

One must possess the basic *motivation* and *determination* to improve his or her position.

When it comes to "how to use what'cha got," your own *"Want To"* and *"Will Do"* make all the difference in the world. The person in Solomon's kingdom who was not highly motivated probably felt extremely uncomfortable.

> Take a lesson from the ants, you lazy fellow. Learn from their ways and be wise! For though they have no king to make them work, yet they

labor hard all summer, gathering food for the winter. But you—all you do is sleep. When will you wake up? "Let me sleep a little longer!" Sure, just a little more! And as you sleep, poverty creeps upon you like a robber and destroys you; want attacks you in full armor (Prov. 6:6-11, TLB).

A wise youth makes hay while the sun shines, but what a shame to see a lad who sleeps away his hour of opportunity (Prov. 10:5, TLB).

Hard work brings prosperity; playing around brings poverty (Prov. 28:19, TLB).

Solomon knew that there was no substitute for *diligence, drive,* and *determination.* He was fully aware that motivation was a basic characteristic of the successful.

Solomon's Success MODEL

M **Motivation**—One must possess the basic *motivation and determination* to improve his or her position

O **Overview** —One must possess the ability to see the big picture as to where he or she is, where he or she wants to be, and how he or she plans to get there

D **Decisions** —One must possess the ability to *make decisions*

E **Education** —One must possess the ability and perception of the need to *accumulate the understanding of certain basic concepts*

L **Look** —One must possess the ability to *look beyond* the immediate and deal with *real value*

O—Overview

One must possess the ability to see the big picture as to where he or she is, where he or she wants to be, and how he or she plans to get there.

Once you determine *where you are,* it is important to establish your goals as to *where you want to be.* But that is not sufficient. You must then engineer a *plan to get there.* All three of these factors are important, and they must be kept in balance with each other. An overemphasis on *where you are* could lead you to discouragement or a sense of false security. An overbalance on *where you want to be* could

82

render you a little schizoid. A preoccupation with a *plan to get there* will frustrate you and tempt you to take a lot of shortcuts.

> Riches can disappear fast. And the king's crown doesn't stay in his family forever—so watch your business interests closely. *Know the state of your flocks and your herds; then there will be* lamb's wool *enough* for clothing, and goat's milk *enough* for food for all your household after the *hay is harvested,* and the new *crop appears,* and the mountain grasses are *gathered in* (Prov. 27:23-27, TLB, emphasis added).

> A sensible man watches for problems ahead and prepares to meet them. The simpleton never looks, and suffers the consequences (Prov. 27:12, TLB).

D—Decisions

One must possess the ability to *make decisions.*

There are many reasons for people being indecisive:
- fear of being wrong
- not willing to accept the responsibility
- afraid of criticism
- insufficient facts
- someone more dominant has always made their decisions for them
- lack of self-esteem

. . . and many other individual reasons. But Solomon shows us that there need be no fear in being decisive.

> He shows how to distinguish right from wrong, *how to find the right decision every time* (Prov. 2:9, TLB, emphasis added).

I have yet to meet a person who is afraid of making a *right* decision. Fear is tied to the perceived results of a wrong decision. Practice the mind of Christ in your decision making, and you will eliminate the fear of uncertainty. Solomon, I am sure, would agree wholeheartedly with the apostle Paul, who claims:

> But the spiritual man has insight into everything, and that bothers and baffles the man of the world, who can't understand him at all. How could he? For certainly he has never been one to know the Lord's thoughts, or to discuss them with him, or to move the hands of God by prayer. *But, strange as it seems, we Christians actually do have within us a portion of the very thoughts and mind of Christ* (I Cor. 2:15, 16, TLB, emphasis added).

E—Education

One must possess the ability and perception of the need to *accumulate the understanding of certain basic concepts.*

It is a little frightening when you realize that accumulated knowledge is now doubling every few years. To be successful, you must remain informed. There must be a *desire* to understand. For that very reason you were directed to spend a considerable amount of time in Chapter Four learning about money, the Federal Reserve system, taxation, the national debt, and inflation. Solomon declares,

> The intelligent man is always open to new ideas. In fact, he looks for them (Prov. 18:15, TLB).

> Get the facts at any price, and hold on tightly to all the good sense you can get (Prov. 23:23, TLB).

> Any enterprise is built by wise planning, becomes strong through common sense, and profits wonderfully by keeping abreast of the facts (Prov. 24:3, 4, TLB).

L—Look

One must possess the ability to *look beyond* the immediate and deal with *real value.*

Much has been written of late about the subject of *clarifying our values.* Possession of this characteristic ability has always been, and always will be, of extreme importance to the successful. It deals with alternatives, selection, priorities, qualities. It's the ability to tell the difference between *fool's gold* and the *real stuff!*

> Trust in your money and down you go! Trust in God and flourish as a tree! (Prov. 11:28, TLB).

> The man who wants to do right will get a rich reward. But the man who wants to get rich quick will quickly fail (Prov. 28:20, TLB).

We will be dealing with this ability in the final chapters of our study as we investigate the possibility of untangling our emotions from the concept of the "dollar" so that we can deal with real values.

There was once a wise old theologian by the name of John Wesley. He was the founding father of the great Methodist movement. When asked for his advice regarding the economy, he summed it all up by crisply saying: *"Earn all you can. Save all you can. Give all you can."*

We will use his advice as a format for the last three chapters in this section:

HOW TO USE WHAT'CHA GOT
EARN ALL YOU CAN
SAVE ALL YOU CAN
GIVE ALL YOU CAN

6
Earn All You Can

INTRODUCTION

One of Solomon's wise observations was discussed earlier: "The good man's earnings advance the cause of righteousness" (Prov. 10:16a, TLB). I am more convinced today than ever that God enjoys blessing His children with specific, individual help with their *earnings*. I can testify to many, many occasions where business transactions were put together, not because of personal intelligence or experience but because God brought together all the pieces of the business puzzle and then gave the divine insights as to how it should all fit together.

For the Christian, to give is gracious, but to gain is also good. *Increased earnings* may be a part of your future ministry.

> For God, who gives seed to the farmer to plant, and later on, good crops to harvest and eat, will give you more and more seed to plant and will make it grow *so that you can give away more and more fruit from your harvest* (II Cor. 9:10, TLB, emphasis added).
>
> For the man who uses well what he is given shall be given more, and he shall have abundance (Mt. 25:29a, TLB).
>
> *It is possible to give away and become richer!* It is also possible to hold on too tightly and lose everything. Yes, the liberal man shall be rich! By watering others, he waters himself (Prov. 11:24, 25, TLB, emphasis added).

Let's find out how you can earn all you can in the following five areas:

I. YOUR GOALS

As you learned in Solomon's Success Model, God is under no obligation to bless and increase the position of the lazy or uncommitted. God wants you to *work hard, set goals, dream dreams,* and *make specific plans* for the future. Solomon said, "We should make plans—counting on God to direct us" (Prov. 16:9, TLB).

God designed you to be a goal-oriented creature. You pursue accomplishment much like the bird pursues the building of a nest. Have you ever observed the amazing activities of a bird in spring? No one has to tell the bird where to build the nest or how to build the nest. Still, it engineers its construction like a master craftsman. The bird also knows the exact date when the construction project must be completed in order to house the young.

Just as the bird sets out to accomplish its goal of building its nest, so you pursue the accomplishment of your specific goals, you will move toward those goals with systematic certainty and purpose.

But what happens if your goals have never become specific? What if you have never clearly defined your goals so that your subconscious mind can concentrate all of its energies on accomplishing them? Or, what if you have instructed your subconscious mind to attain unworthy, improper, or inconsistent goals? The old adage insists that *if you don't know where you are going, any road will get you there.*

Since God created you to be such a goal-oriented creature, you are usually at your height of happiness and self-esteem when your goals are consistent and clearly defined, and when you are positively engaged in an active pursuit of your worthwhile goals. Therefore, let's investigate the five basic functions in goal setting and achievement:

FANTASIZE
CRYSTALIZE
VISUALIZE
VERBALIZE
MATERIALIZE

A. Fantasize

You personally hold the key to how much you earn. You are the only one who ultimately determines what you will do with the possessions in your personal portfolio. Don't be afraid to dream! No one accomplishes a thing *in fact* that he does not first accomplish *in his mind*. If you wish to earn more, you must dream more. One of the most astounding exercises you can practice is to stand tall, look squarely into the face of the future and say, "What if . . . ?" Never look back and say: *What if . . . ?* That will lead to negative fantasizing, discouragement, and will ultimately drive you batty. But rather, shake from your mind those shackles that would bind your present creativity, and stir to life new dreams from buried hopes.

I was greatly affected the other day as Dr. Bill Bright, my brother David, and I sat together in Denver having lunch. Dr. Bright shared with us the way that God had allowed him to begin dreaming of souls being brought into the Kingdom. First it was 1, then 10, then 100, then 1,000, then 100,000, then one million! As he dared to dream, God dared to dispense miracle after miracle. Has he stopped dreaming? Oh, no! The present dream . . . *one billion* souls born into the Kingdom of God!

Every achievement must first be a vivid mental image projected on the screen of your mind. God is eager to disclose His creativity through the receptive imaginations of His children.

In your notebook list your dreams. These may be old dreams or brand-new ones. Don't judge your dreams at this point, just write them down. Write them down as if there were no limitations. Write your dream for each category.

  I. My Financial Dreams:
 II. My Personal Dreams: *physical, intellectual, emotional, volitional* (decision-making characteristics), *and temporal* (my time).
III. My Relational Dreams: *family, friends, and influence.*
IV. My Spiritual Dreams:
 V. Dreams About My Special Abilities & Talents:
VI. Additional Personal Dreams:

B. Crystalize

It was important for you to write down your dreams, *for in your dreams you will find your goals.* Your dreams dare not remain vague or general. They must become specific. For only then can you begin to determine whether or not they are worthy of becoming *crystalized goals.*

The process of *dream screening* includes the implementation of your *priorities and values.*

1. What will it cost to attain this dream?
2. If you allowed this dream to become a crystalized goal, would it be consistent with your other goals?
3. Would this dream be consistent with God's Word?
4. If the dream were to become a specific goal, would the time and

energy invested to see its attainment cause God to smile or frown?
5. How does your mate relate to the dream?

These and other questions must be asked as you sort through your dreams and determine your *crystalized goals.*

Go back now to your list of dreams and apply your techniques of dream screening. First identify which goals are long range (15-20 years), which are short range (five to ten years), and which are immediate (six months). Then, using a separate page for each goal, and beginning with the most long range, answer *each* of the screening questions for *each* goal.

As you learned in Solomon's Success Model, the ultimate achievers are those who can realistically say: Here I am today, this is where I intend to be tomorrow, this is how I intend to get from here to there! To visualize this, let's look at the financial area. The chances are fairly certain that you will not earn more unless you have some crystalized reason for earning it.

Perhaps one of your long-range goals included money enough for retirement. Following is a handy formula by which you can calculate the retirement income you will need.

Calculate the Retirement Income You Will Need:

(1) Yearly after-tax retirement income
    needed in today's dollars: _____

(2) Known future retirement income from
    Social Security, company or individual
    retirement plans _____

    Average rate of inflation anticipated
    until retirement _____

(3) Number of years until retirement _____

(4) Inflation factor based on inflation rate
    and years until retirement (see table) _____

_____ x _____ = _____
   (1) - (2)   (4)   Additional Annual Income Needed for Retirement

C. Visualize

It was stated earlier that no one accomplishes a thing in fact that he does not first accomplish in his mind. That not only holds true for the dreaming aspect of goal setting, but it is true in the *visualizing* of the *attainment* of that goal. You must be able to see yourself as having already accomplished it.

I have always liked to listen to the old saints of the church. As they get closer to physical death, they begin to identify more and more

Additional Income Needed (in Dollars) at Retirement, with Various Inflation Rates

Years Until Retirement	5%	Rate of Inflation 8%	10%	12%
1	1.05	1.08	1.10	1.12
2	1.10	1.17	1.21	1.25
3	1.16	1.26	1.33	1.40
4	1.22	1.36	1.46	1.57
5	1.28	1.47	1.61	1.76
6	1.34	1.59	1.77	1.97
7	1.41	1.71	1.95	2.21
8	1.48	1.85	2.14	2.48
9	1.55	2.00	2.36	2.77
10	1.63	2.16	2.59	3.11
11	1.71	2.33	2.85	3.48
12	1.80	2.52	3.14	3.90
13	1.89	2.72	3.45	4.36
14	1.98	2.94	3.80	4.89
15	2.08	3.17	4.18	5.47
16	2.18	3.43	4.60	6.13
17	2.29	3.70	5.05	6.87
18	2.41	4.00	5.56	7.69
19	2.53	4.32	6.12	8.61
20	2.65	4.66	6.73	9.65
21	2.79	5.03	7.40	10.80
22	2.93	5.44	8.14	12.10
23	3.07	5.87	8.95	13.55
24	3.23	6.34	9.85	15.18
25	3.39	6.85	10.83	17.00
26	3.56	7.40	11.92	19.04
27	3.73	7.99	13.11	21.32
28	3.92	8.63	14.42	23.88
29	4.12	9.32	15.86	26.75
30	4.32	10.06	17.45	29.96
31	4.54	10.87	19.19	33.56
32	4.76	11.74	21.11	37.58
33	5.00	12.68	23.23	42.09
34	5.25	13.69	25.55	47.14
35	5.52	14.79	28.10	52.80

with their future role in Heaven. They begin to talk about what they will do, whom they will see, and what the Crystal River will actually look like. Pop Jackson in the last hours of consciousness requested that his hospital bed be turned toward the doorway so that he would be able to see Jesus come through the door to take him to Heaven. He was totally identifying with his goal. He could actually picture himself in the arms of Jesus!

It is important for you to be able to visualize yourself in the position of attainment. If you want to be a skier, you must first know in your mind that you *can* ski. Then you can begin visualizing the actual techniques of posture, balance control, and weight shifting necessary to the sport. You then must practice those techniques over and over. But it is important for you to be able to visualize yourself in a position of attaining them long enough for the subconscious mind to work out the details of actual coordination and accomplishment.

D. Verbalize

The *verbalizing* of your goals acts as a positive reinforcement. This verbalization should be *to God, to yourself,* and *to someone else.*

First, be sure that you share your dreams and goals *verbally with God* in prayer. He wants you to talk to Him about them and to ask Him for His advice and guidance. Be sensitive then and quick to respond to any insights or commands that He gives to you. After all, remember that He has the *ultimate interest* in your goals since *He really owns all the possessions in your portfolio anyway!*

Secondly, it is important to verbalize your goals to yourself. That can be done through *positive verbal affirmations.* Positive verbal affirmations are simply statements of truth that tend to reinforce your goals. They will reinforce your personal attitude and strengthen your confidence. The power of a verbal affirmation is astounding. But *make sure that the direction in which you tell yourself to head is indeed the direction you want to go.* For as you program direction and destination into your subconscious mind, it will amaze you how surely and how quickly you will arrive. "For as he thinketh in his heart, so is he" (Prov. 23:7, KJV).

Thirdly, find friends in whom you have confidence and tell them your dreams and specific crystalized goals. Ask them for advice. Let them be your sounding board. Talk about your goals; get them out into the open. You will be amazed at your new perspective and your new insights into how you can achieve those goals. Sharing your dreams and goals with your mate, friends, or family will create a very strong bond of trust and appreciation. Don't worry about ridicule or misunderstanding. Become vulnerable.

Additionally, there is a sense of *accountability* that goes along with verbalizing your goals to someone else. Inquiry can be made periodically as to your progress, which may be just the encouragement you need to keep you on track.

E. Materialize

The materialization of your goal is the process whereby your goal actually *becomes reality*. Once you have dreamed and screened, crystalized, visualized, and verbalized your goals, you can then begin applying the habits, attitudes, and actions necessary for those dreams to become reality. You can begin implementing your plan of action for their accomplishment.

Occasionally you will encounter obstacles—roadblocks in your pathway of pursuit. Your attitude will determine how you handle those obstacles. You will allow those roadblocks to become either your *tombstone* or your *touchstone*.

If you allow your obstacles to control you and permanently reroute you from your pathway of accomplishment, the chances are good that the result will be frustrated suppression of the instinct to accomplish, and your attitude will be characterized by cynicism, bitterness, hopelessness, and a low self-esteem. But through God's ingenious creativity and grace, those obstacles can be surmounted, and even negative opinions of others can simply become the fuel that helps propel your rocketship on toward accomplishment.

As each goal is attained, a personal feeling of accomplishment will grow and your feeling of worthwhileness will blossom. As you strive toward accomplishing your goals, you will begin to recognize your own potential as your relate to God's master plan. Your perspective will be better and your creativity will increase.

Remember: *You are usually at your height of happiness and self-esteem when your goals are consistent and clearly defined, and when you are positively engaged in an active pursuit of your worthwhile goals.*

II. YOUR JOB

A. Your Present Job

The Kingdom is advanced through the earnings of the good man or woman. The good person's financial earnings come primarily through a job. He or she takes some possessions from his or her portfolio, i.e., *time* and *abilities*, and trades them to an employer for a paycheck. It is intended that you will work. Paul told the church at Thessalonica, "Even while we were still there with you we gave you this rule: 'He who does not work shall not eat'" (II Thess. 3:10, TLB). You'll need that paycheck to fulfill many of those personal goals previously listed. So, the subject of your job is an important one.

Before continuing, let's find out *where you are*, presently. In your notebook write out your present job description. Give details on location, position, description of work activities, for how long, and why you work there.

Then, determine your monthly *Take-Home Pay* from your present job. To this amount add all other sources of spendable family income calculated on a monthly basis: your spouse's take-home pay, net rental income, dividends or royalties, etc. This will show you your total average monthly spendable income.

Have you ever wondered about your earning ability compared to your age? The following diagram portrays the average American's pattern of earning throughout his life. Would you agree that your life fits this pattern?

AVERAGE AMERICAN LIFE LINE

B. Jobs in the Future

Solomon realized the importance of your job:

> Well, one thing, at least, is good: it is for a man to . . . accept his position in life, and enjoy his work whatever his job may be, for however long the Lord may let him live.
>
> And, of course, it is very good if a man has received wealth from the Lord, and the good health to enjoy it. To enjoy your work and to accept your lot in life—that is indeed a gift from God. The person who does that will not need to look back with sorrow on his past, for God gives him joy (Eccl. 5:18-20, TLB).

At the beginning of the 1980s there were more than 95 million job holders in the United States. An alarmingly high percentage of those workers were deeply discontented with their everyday work lives. They felt they had little or nothing to say about the work assigned to them; their opinions and recommendations were not welcomed; and there was little or no possibility for the feeling of personal achievement or appreciation.

As you might suspect, that problem affects more than just the worker. The attitude of the unhappy worker spreads out to the issue of productivity. *Productivity* is one of the prime essentials in curbing *inflation* which, as you learned in Chapter Four, greatly influences the economic stability of the country.

In your notebook describe your "dream job." List as many details as possible including job description, compensation, location, and any other elements.

Perhaps this will come to you as a shock: If you are an average American male or female 20 years old, you can expect to make more than six job changes during the remainder of your working life. Even if you are 40, you can still expect to make more than two job changes. And even at 50, don't be surprised if you find yourself making at least one more job change.

No longer does the average person think of choosing an occupation in terms of one great, giant decision. But rather, it is more of a continuous process. Your current choices will create your continuous career. Technological advances can destroy old careers, as well as create new ones. Today's young worker may not just change jobs several times, but there is a strong likelihood that he may have at least three different careers. The changing needs and desires of the American society affect the types of jobs available. And your exposure to those changes, plus our access to training and educational opportunities, will largely affect your choices.

More and more training is being required of the worker, but not necessarily college training. The Bureau of Labor Statistics predicts that the number of college graduates entering the work force will exceed openings in jobs that college graduates have traditionally filled by 2.7 million in the next decade. Does this imply that you should no longer encourage your children to go to college? No, not at all. But it does mean that college is not necessarily for everyone, and the lack of a college degree is not something of which to be ashamed. Today a new respect is being created for the technically skilled craftsman.

Even though a college degree is no longer a guarantee for employment, the pay for the college graduate who can find work will remain somewhat higher, and it will still take a degree to get to the very top. (You may be interested in obtaining your own *Occupational Outlook Handbook* from the Superintendent of Documents, United States Government Printing Office, Washington, DC 20210.)

C. How to Get a Job

If you are just getting out of high school or college, or if your present position is demanding a job change, or if you're a woman who is determined to return to an outside job, there are several things you can do that will be of aid to you.

If you have already conscientiously filled out your Personal

Portfolio in Chapter Two, completed the section on "Your Goals," and filled out the information regarding your "Present Job" and "Dream Job," you will have no problem compiling an *Employment Inventory* of yourself. In your notebook make a list of information that will include the following areas:

1. Your abilities, talents, and skills
2. Your work history
3. Your physical condition
4. Your nonwork activities, e.g., hobbies, volunteer jobs, leadership roles in your church, etc.
5. Your marital status
6. Your education
7. Your financial status
8. Your goals for your career

From this *Employment Inventory* you will be able to write a comprehensive *Resumé*. Be very selective and concise when you write your resumé. Select carefully the facts that you include, remembering that a resumé is your way of "selling yourself" and your abilities to our future boss. Never make your resumé more than two pages long, and be sure it is neatly typed or typeset even if you must have someone else prepare it for you!

Be prepared to add *references* to your resumé if requested. Be sure to get people's permission before you use them as references.

You should rewrite your resumé at least five or six times. Leave it for a couple of days and then go back and do it one more time.

If you would like some help in writing your resumé, you may write to the U.S. Department of Labor, Manpower Administration, Washington, D.C. 20210, and ask for their publication, *"Merchandising Your Job Talents."*

When applying for a job, don't go in and ask for "just any kind of job y'all got open." Be specific. Be sure that you never criticize your former employer, and never volunteer information regarding any financial or domestic problem that you may be having. Never be deceptive about yourself or your abilities, but put your "best foot forward."

There are several factors that will nearly guarantee a *"REJECTION"* stamp to be placed on an application:
- Unsatisfactory personal appearance
- Passive or indifferent attitude, lack of interest or enthusiasm
- Poor self-expression, i.e., voice, diction, grammar
- Overemphasis on money
- Attitude that someone "owes" you something

- Unsatisfactory scholastic record
- Expects too much too soon, an unwillingness to start at the bottom

D. The Woman on the Job

There is a 90 percent chance that if you are a woman between the ages of 18 and 75, you will work or have worked at a paying job for a prolonged span at some time during your life. In fact, the odds are more than 50-50 that you are presently working at such a job. Very few things have ever affected the Gross National Product of the United States quite like the women going to work. There appears to be absolutely no reversing the trend of increasing numbers of women on the job. It is estimated today that a woman will work at a paying job for at least 25 years of her life.

Of course, many women work because they have to. They must work in order to help meet the financial needs of the family. In today's economy of runaway inflation, that is becoming more and more the case. It is ideal if the mother can avoid working outside the home while the children are in their preschool years. Those are important years for Mom and the kids to be together.

But not all women work because they have to work. Many work purely for the personal fulfillment. The children are in school, a lot of yesteryear-type household chores are lightened by automation and technology, and they are sick and tired of just sitting at home being entertained by daytime television. They want to feel like worthwhile individuals who can still make a contribution.

An interesting phenomenon that is characteristic of our modern society is *the empty nest*. The empty nest is where both parents are still alive but the last child has left home. Years ago many families never really knew an empty nest. Families would be large and the child-bearing years would be well extended, so that by the time the last child was ready to leave home, one or the other of the parents would have already died. But today, because of longer life spans, smaller families, and childbearing that usually is concluded earlier, the empty nest is becoming very common. It is now very possible for a couple to spend 25 to 30 years together in an empty nest.

The homemaker in this category is the exception. It would be advisable for you to plan ahead for the empty nest. Even if you are a mother currently at home with the kids, it would be a good idea to acquire enough education to qualify you for the type of job you would like to hold during those later years and keep those skills up to date.

E. Some Career Guides for the Would-be Executive

Sylvia Porter passes on several helpful hints that have molded the careers of some famous industrialists.

(1) In the first five years of your job career—say, from age 22 to 28—try to find out what you want to do, what you want to be. Don't hesitate to make several job changes, for you are testing yourself. As a young man or woman, ask yourself: "What do I want out of life? What do I want to do?"

In these years young men or women who are unmarried are generally more successful than married individuals, because they can more easily move around on their own and more easily be moved by their firms.

(2) Also, in the 22 to 28 age range, concentrate on finding the industry in which you want to stay. The future top leaders are to an impressive extent the ones who were set in their own industry in their twenties and who then moved within it to gain know-how.

(3) At the age of 30, stop and think hard. Take the time to sit down quietly and write out some answers to yourself on such questions as these:

Where do you want to live? Where would you and your spouse be happiest? How much annual pay will you need to earn ten or fifteen years from now to meet the standard of living you want?

You'll have a much clearer concept of your goals after you've honestly made this effort to "know thyself"—which well may be among the hardest tasks you'll ever undertake.

(4) For the next ten years—say, to age 40—prepare yourself deliberately for what you want to be. Grade yourself on these qualities for success: drive, responsibility, health, good character, ability to communicate, ability to think, ability to get along with people, ability to keep your perspectives (i.e., recognize your responsibilities to society even while you're watching your competitors in business).

(5) In the 40 to 42 age bracket you'll hit a treacherous phase of "cyclical restlessness" when you may mistakenly change jobs because you're looking for the "greener grass." Be on guard: again, quietly check up on your goals.

(6) After age 45 start consolidating—use the years to broaden your objectives, achieve fulfillment, lay the basis for a rewarding new life after you leave your company (*Sylvia Porter's New Money Book for the '80's.* © 1975, 1979 by Sylvia Porter. Reprinted by permission of Doubleday & Co.).

Your job is important. Be sure you act wisely when it comes to trading your time and talent for that periodic paycheck.

III. YOUR INVESTMENTS

In addition to your regular job it is very likely that you will receive earnings throughout your life as a result of wise investments. In Christ's Parable of the Talents in Matthew 25:14-29, those who were given talents were expected to invest them wisely so that they would bring an increase. The one who *failed to invest* was charged with being "wicked" and "lazy" (TLB).

Investment information is given quite generously through the Bible. Warnings are given to those who would take shortcuts and yield to the temptation of the "get-rich-quick" schemes.

> The man who wants to do right will get a rich reward. But the man who wants to get rich quick will quickly fail (Prov. 28:20, TLB).

> Steady plodding brings prosperity; hasty speculation brings poverty (Prov. 21:5, TLB).

> A fortune can be made from cheating, but there is a curse that goes with it (Prov. 20:21, TLB).

> There is another serious problem I have seen everywhere—savings are put into risky investments that turn sour, and soon there is nothing left to pass on to one's son. The man who speculates is soon back to where he began—with nothing. This, as I said, is a very serious problem, for all his hard work has been for nothing; he has been working for the wind. It is all swept away. All the rest of his life he is under a cloud—gloomy, discouraged, frustrated, and angry (Eccl. 5:13-17, TLB).

Even a sound, consistent investment strategy can become discouraging at times, especially when you are not seeing immediate results. That is when you are to take courage and . . . and keep at it! "Keep on sowing your seed, for you never know which will grow—perhaps it all will" (Eccl. 11: 6, TLB).

A. Your Investment Options

This is not an all-inclusive list, but it will give you a little start. To this list you need to add our own individual investment options and begin doing personal research on those areas.

1. YOUR HOME

Your home will probably be the biggest single investment you will make in your lifetime. Also, the mortgage you take on to finance it is likely to be the biggest single debt of your life. But, if you invest wisely, the value in your home is virtually certain to grow over the years. Today a home is a great hedge against inflation. As the value of the dollar decreases, you will get more dollars out of your home if you ever sell it.

During *periods of economic inflation* it makes sense to tender as small a down payment as possible, take out a mortgage as long as possible, and retire the debt with dollars of steadily depreciating value. You can pay the loan back with "cheap dollars."

If a young couple seems frightened by the rates charged for interest these days, I usually try to help them understand how to figure the *real rate of interest.* The real rate of interest is the rate of interest being charged minus the rate of inflation. For instance, if the interest being charged for financing the home is ten percent, and the rate of inflation is six percent, then the *real rate of interest* is four percent.

One of the increasing problems in today's economy is that it is becoming more and more difficult to qualify to buy a home. The traditional rule of thumb has been that the family's gross income should be at least five times its mortgage payment. In 1950, seven out of ten families could qualify. Today, less than four out of ten U.S. families can qualify, and it is becoming more difficult each month.

Another old rule of thumb is that you can afford to buy a house costing roughly two and one half times your gross yearly income. For example, if your annual gross income is $40,000, you can afford a home in the $90,000 to $100,000 bracket.

In the present market many lenders and borrowers have ignored those standards of affordability. The scene has become more complicated. The more difficult it has become to buy a home, the more determined some couples have become in making the purchase. Some are holding off having babies so that they can devote more of their income to a down payment. Some are returning back to school to prepare themselves for job promotions. The purchasing of a home has become as source of motivation for the wife to go to work even if it is just long enough for her salary to help them qualify for the loan. I do not recommend using unwise methods to secure a mortgage. But if you can qualify to buy a home, you can be quite confident that your investment will be both stable and high-yielding.

Not only are you able to hedge against inflation and take advantage of value appreciation, but there are some tax benefits in owning as opposed to renting.

There are other emotional and social advantages to investing in your own home. Do not be discouraged if you cannot buy your own home, but do not hesitate to purchase if you have the chance.

2. THE STOCK MARKET

The concept of the stock market is almost symbolic of the free enterprise system in the United States. If you desire to own a share of common stock in a U.S. publicly held corporation, you may do so. If you do, you then own part of the corporation along with all the other shareholders—whether it is General Motors, IBM, or General Electric. Many people think that "investing" is exclusively synonymous with buying shares of stock through a stockbroker.

It must be understood that the Dow-Jones Industrial Average (DJIA) or Standard & Poor's Corporate Index of 500 Stocks (S & P's

50—the most widely accepted standard of overall market performance) are no more than *just averages*. And the "average" does not exclude the possibility of an individual stock success. In fact, almost everyone believes that he can beat the averages.

It is true that things began to turn around in the mid-80s for the stock market. The Dow Jones Industrials ran up an impressive 24 percent in 1986, over 20 percent in 1987 and that was on top of an amazing 29 percent in 1985. For the first time in history the D.J.I. went over the 2200 mark. The boom was spurred by what looked like low inflation, strong monetary growth, low interest, and a lower dollar. The bullish run was also aided by eager foreign investors who pumped in at least $26 billion into American shares in 1986 alone.

Another factor influencing the upturn was the painful reorganizing and retrenching that American corporations had just gone through which had made them leaner and meaner and more profitable. In the majority of cases the corporate assets were truly undervalued. That made them very attractive

The rules of the stock market have changed over the years. A generation ago investors were advised to buy high quality stocks and sit back and collect the interest and dividends for the next 20 or 30 years. Today that won't work. Yesterday's golden opportunity could be tomorrow's financial disaster. If you are determined to invest in the current market, you must either be willing to pay for expert money management or be willing to pay the price to become a pro yourself. If you don't become a pro yourself, then don't try to beat the professional traders who today are equipped with rows of computers and rooms of technicians. By the time you think you can spot a trend with the naked eye, rest assured that a financial robot already spotted it earlier, responded, and altered its significance.

Now that you have been sufficiently frightened by the market negatives, let me confuse you by reaffirming the importance of the stock market concept as it relates to free enterprise and offer you a few helpful hints for stock market investing:

- *Invest in the stock market only after you have sufficiently taken care of emergency provisions that would help you through an unexpected financial upset. If you do not have that extra available cushion, then you cannot afford to invest in stocks. Your losses should be affordable.*
- *Even though stocks are relatively liquid, you should not invest more than 20 percent of your assets in stocks, even if you can buy a bargain.*
- *Don't buy or sell stocks just because it seems the thing to do; i.e., stock market "conforming" doesn't pay off.*
- *Don't buy stocks of a type or in amounts that would keep you from sleeping well. Anxiety and concern should not be a part of your stock*

game. If you are so nervous about owning stocks that you can't take a trip with the family without worrying about what is happening to your stocks, stay out of the market.

3. REAL ESTATE

You may feel after reading this section that the author is slightly prejudiced *toward* investments in real estate. The only problem with that statement is the usage of the word "slightly," because real estate *has been* the vehicle God has used to fulfill many of our personal dreams. However, hopefully, I will still be able to fairly present *the virtues* and *the pitfalls* of real estate investment.

a. *Some Basic Concepts*

The great financial giant, Andrew Carnegie, was quoted as saying that of all the highly wealthy men he had known, the vast majority had accumulated their wealth in one way or another through land and the profits that land could produce.

The population of the earth requires a certain amount of land from which to derive all products. Therefore, so long as the population of the earth increases and the amount of the land stays the same, the value of land, in general, will increase due to the increase in demand.

Some land, however, might only increase 15 percent per year in value, while other land might increase 200 percent in one year. The deciding difference will be found as you answer the following three questions: *Where* is the land located? *How* can the land be used? *What* are the financial terms?

(1) *Where is the land and how can it be used?*

There are certain basic demands that create the highest appreciation upon the price of land.

- *The demand of oil, strategic metals, or other valuable commodities found within the ground.* I have seen a very small piece of ground sell for an unbelievable amount of money if it was needed for a mine shaft or a drilling rig.
- *The demand for urban and suburban residential and business developments.* Over 70 percent of our expanding population continues to congregate in the nation's major metropolitan areas. Environmental concerns and government regulations will drive the prices up in areas that are already developed since it will be increasingly difficult to develop new areas. Properties with available services, e.g., utilities, water taps, gas taps, sewer taps, etc., will no doubt realize accelerated prices at historical rates. Due to energy shortages there will probably be a move to redevelop city properties.

- *The demand for industrial land,* which would include land along major transportation routes, i.e., railroads, seaports, rivers, and freeways. Properly zoned land around airports will continue to increase in value for industrial parks and freight depots.
- *The demand for land to be farmed.* Prices for good farmland have increased by leaps and bounds. As the population increases, there are more mouths to be fed. Another sad but true factor that has increased the price of farmland has been the takeover of the small family farm by the large farming corporations.
- *The demand for recreational land.* Land around ski areas, new lakes, on fishing streams, areas adjacent to national forests or parks, areas that have ocean frontage or border on other water bodies have shown and will continue to show some of the sharpest increases in value. Recreation land should be within three—no more than five—hours driving time from the metropolitan area.

(2) *What are the financial terms?*

No matter how good a piece of real estate may be, you can still lose money on it if you initially pay too much for it, or if you cannot live with the terms. But there are still bargains to be had. It is very possible that some of those bargains are right in your neighborhood: diamonds in your own backyard. Just because you are required to pay the present market price for a piece of property does not exclude it from being a bargain. The most substantial bargains are often found in the terms, i.e., amount of down payment, length of mortgage life, possibility of assuming a low-interest loan, or the possibility of the owner "carrying back" the mortgage himself, thereby eliminating loan "fees," mortgagee's policies, etc.

One of the most important concepts regarding real estate is the *principle of leverage.* Quite simply, leverage is where you can put down a little and control a lot. There is great benefit to you if you are able to borrow between 70 to 80 percent of the cost of a piece of property and thus tie up only a small amount of your own capital. For example, suppose you invested in a $10,000 parcel of land with a $2,500 down payment. Suppose you then secured a mortgage for the $7,500 balance at 10 percent interest per year amortized over 20 years. Let's say that you then were able to resell the property after two years for $15,000—a very realistic achievement.

During those two years your monthly mortgage payments of $72.38 per month would have amounted to $1,737.12. You would have paid off $262.50 in principal and the balance of $1,474.62 would have been your interest cost. Your net profit on the deal would have been $3,526 ($15,000 − $11,474) . . . *but* your total outlay would have been just $4,237.12. *That's an 85 percent profit in only two years.*

If you own your own home and that home has a mortgage on it, you are taking advantage of the principle of leverage. When you use leverage, you are utilizing the principle of OPM (Other People's Money). When you purchased that property, the down payment was your own money, but the balance was OPM. The *interest* you pay is simply rent on OPM. When you utilize OPM, you are allowed to control the entire property rather than just the portion represented by your own money.

In the example concerning the $10,000 piece of ground, you were able to understand how the principles of leverage and OPM are used in investing in raw land. The principles are the same when applied to investing in income-producing property, only sometimes they work out even more dramatically. It is possible to purchase a million-dollar apartment complex with a 20-25 percent down payment. Instead of just earning an income from your 20-25 percent that you used as down payment, you would now control, and begin earning, on the total million-dollar complex.

It is possible to take the commodity known as "money" and make it work for you. The financially independent people that I know today or have read about in history all used in one form or another the principle of OPM. Of course, you can abuse the principles . . . but not for very long. Remember: *He is broken by the laws of credit who tries to break the laws of credit.*

You certainly do not want to use OPM for things that decrease in value but rather for things that are going to *increase* in value.

b. *Disadvantages to Investing in Real Estate*
  (1) *Property Taxes:* Increases in property taxes are being experienced everywhere. They are a cost of real estate ownership.
  (2) *High Interest Rates:* High interest rates on mortgages become a significant factor in purchasing real estate.
  (3) *General Economic Influence:* During periods of recession or depression, values of certain types of real estate are affected, e.g., some recreational areas.

(4) *Front-end Investment:* In order to get into real estate, it usually takes a significant amount of money for the down payment.

(5) *Liquidity:* Real estate is not the most liquid of the investment options. It may take months to dispose of a property at your desired price. In the stock market, you can usually have your money the next day.

(6) *Commissions:* In today's market, if you engage the help of a real estate company to dispose of your property, you can expect to pay from seven percent to ten percent or more of the total selling price.

(7) *No Formal Market:* When it comes to buying and selling real estate, there is no formal market as there is in trading securities. You cannot simply pick up your newspaper and determine the value of an investment across the country.

c. *Summary of Advantages to Investing in Real Estate*

(1) *Return:* Proven to be a sound, long-term investment with relatively high rewards and relatively low risks. An increase in real estate values means someone is going to make a profit.

(2) *Tax Advantages:* Profits made in real estate have in the past enjoyed favorable tax treatment. If you meet certain qualifications interest and depreciation are still deductible and proceeds from the sale of real property can be protected.

(3) *Inflation Hedge:* Real estate stays relative to the economy. In addition, you have the advantage during inflationary times to borrow "expensive" dollars and pay them back with dollars that are becoming increasingly "cheap."

(4) *Leverage and OPM:* You have the opportunity to benefit from being able to control the extended value of a property with a small percentage of down payment.

4. PRECIOUS METALS

Investments in precious metals have increased decidedly in the past few years. Strategic metals with strange-sounding names like indium, tantalum, molybdenum, and columbium are bought and sold today in extensive volume. Most of those metals which are used in technology and industry are purchased by investors who never actually take physical possession of the metals. The investor makes the purchase through the commodity market, arranges to have it warehoused in a bonded location thousands of miles away while he waits for the price to go up; which if it does, affords him a handsome profit on his investment when he resells.

Silver and *gold* also can be bought on the commodities market. But silver and gold enjoy a distinct advantage over other precious metals: they can easily be taken into your personal possession.

Additionally, silver and gold are more commonly recognized and are more easily traded outside the formal marketplace. You may not find many people in your hometown who would be willing to buy 100 ounces of cobalt, but you would be able to find several who would be happy to purchase your gold or silver.

There are several ways to invest in gold and silver. *Purchasing futures contracts through the commodities market* has already been mentioned. Bullion, especially gold, can be purchased and held for you by a Swiss bank. That process is much more simple than you would expect. All you need do is write for information on opening an account.

Bank Leu
Bahnhafstrasse 32
CH 8022 Zurich, Switzerland
Foreign Commerce Bank
Bellariastrasse 82
CH 8030 Zurich, Switzerland

Another way to invest in gold and silver is by *purchasing stock in mining companies.* However, you must keep in mind that when you are investing in stock in a gold or silver company, you are not investing in just the metal, in the truest sense. But rather, you are investing in the company's ability to finance, manage, and operate a business.

I believe that the simplest way to invest in gold or silver is by *purchasing coins that you can personally manage.* There are two types of gold and silver coins that you can buy: *bullion coins* and *numismatic (rare) coins.* I would not personally recommend investing in any of the medallions or small bullions that you see advertised by private mints. The quality and quantity must be authenticated each time you sell or trade, therefore liquidating is more difficult. I would recommend investing in coins that come only from the mint of an established government.

Numismatic (rare) coins can be an exciting investment, and you may realize extraordinary returns, but you must remember that a significant percentage of their value is in their rarity. The rarity factor may be of little value if it ever becomes necessary for you to utilize them in an economic crisis. At such a time, the value will be based on the bullion factor only. The value of bullion coins is determined strictly by the amount of gold or silver contained therein.

a. Silver

There are approximately 235 million ounces of pre-1965 silver coins held by individuals in the Untied States. Those coins contain 90 percent pure silver. In 1964 the U.S. minted the Kennedy half-dollar which was 90 percent silver. But from 1965 to 1970 the silver was reduced to 40 percent in the Kennedy half dollar. Today the U.S. mints copper-clad coins with no silver content. But you can still purchase silver coins. You must, however, pay for the amount of silver content in the coin at today's market price. The coins are purchased in bags weighing approximately 55 pounds, and contain a mixture of pre-1965 dimes, quarters, and half-dollars, with a face amount of the coins totaling $1,000. However, you don't pay $1,000 for the bag of coins. You determine the value of the bag of coins by taking 90 percent of the total weight of the coins (since they are only 90 percent pure silver), which should be approximately 720 ounces, and multiply it by the spot silver price quoted for that day by Handy and Harman in your local newspaper. For example, if the spot price for silver was $10.00 per ounce, the bag would be valued at $7,200. If you insist on buying silver dollars, expect to pay two or three times as much since they are considered rare. I would guess that someday all old silver coins will sell for more than their silver content.

b. Gold

Gold is part of the national wealth reserve of every major country in the world. It is the single store of value that is recognized universally. Historically, a person has been able to readily buy or sell gold in any place in the civilized world. Gold does not rust, tarnish, or corrode. It is virtually indestructible and can be stored for an indefinite period of time. Revolutions come and go, but gold remains. Gold is scarce, yet historically, there has always been an adequate supply to sustain a market. No government has ever been able to successfully regulate gold out of existence. In fact, the more they try to regulate it, the more desire there is for it.

Even if our monetary system moves toward the cashless society, there will always be an underground monetary system that will include gold as its base. In early 1934, the U.S. Government set the price of gold as its base at $35.00 per ounce. You have recently seen gold sell anywhere from $300 to $800 per ounce. I predict that it will eventually reach $1,000 per ounce.

Gold has been called the great "Fear Thermometer." It has been interesting to note that throughout history when people begin to fear the events of the future, they tend to liquidate other assets and turn to gold. When fears subside, gold prices tend to sag.

Though I recommend that every family have some gold and silver coins in their investment portfolio, I do not think that more than ten percent to 15 percent of your assets should ever be represented by precious metals. One reason for this limitation is that even if the gold or silver price stays equal to the rate of inflation, while it is in your possession, it will earn you no interest.

Here are some helpful hints for dealing in precious metals:

- Buy from the most reputable dealer you can find, one who will buy back and is willing to quote you a buy-back price as readily as he will quote you a selling price.
- Check prices with at least three dealers before you buy.
- Take physical delivery of your coins. Don't let someone or some company hold them for you after you purchase them.
- Don't fall for any high leverage or margin schemes in precious metals. Buy when you can afford to pay cash on delivery.
- If you keep your coins in a safe deposit box, make sure you have a joint tenancy agreement with your spouse which covers the coins, and be sure that your spouse has access to a key.
- Don get talked into buying art objects made of gold or silver for your portfolio. You should basically stick to the value of the metal. The same principle applies to investing in minted bars of gold or silver commemorating the moon walk, Mother's Day, Father's Day, or any other day. You usually pay three times as much as the bar's bullion is worth.

5. PRECIOUS GEMSTONES

Gemstones are referred to as a worthy store of wealth throughout the Bible. They have been considered as investment objects for a long time. Diamonds, rubies, sapphires, and emeralds are the four stones that have been historically referred to as precious gemstones. They hold that designation because of their density or hardness. The diamond is the hardest of the four, and the emerald is the least hard.

If you have recently considered the prices of alexandrite, tsavorite, tourmaline, aquamarine, black opal, or cat's-eye chrysoberyl, I'm sure that you are convinced that they all should be considered "precious" just because of their high prices.

But hardness of the stone is not the only thing that divides gems. The greatest economic factor that separates diamonds from colored stones is the tightly controlled market enjoyed by the diamond industry. Virtually all the diamonds of the world are controlled by the Central Selling Organization (CSO), the marketing arm of the DeBeers syndicate. The DeBeers organization controls the diamond industry from the South African or Soviet Union mines to the retail counters of the jewelry stores in your favorite shopping mall. By artfully regulating the supply of diamonds released into the marketplace each year, DeBeers has been able to absolutely dictate the diamond prices. Because of that control, basic diamond prices have not declined at any time in the past 30 years. If they want to increase the prices, they simply do so. Today the diamond industry has become a $12 billion annual business.

a. Diamonds

The "Four Cs" represent the basic characteristics that determine the quality of a diamond: Carat, Color, Clarity, Cut.
The G.I.A. (Gemological Institute of America . . . a nonprofit laboratory with offices in New York and Los Angeles) has done a great deal to clarify the grading standards.

(1) *Carat:* the unit of measurement used to weigh a diamond. A carat is approximately one-fifth of a metric gram. The size of the diamond is always referred to in carats or "points" which are equal to one-hundredth of a carat. An investment stone should be of one carat or more . . . nothing less.

(2) *Color:* (or rather the lack thereof) determines quality. Generally the more yellow in the diamond, the poorer the quality. A scale from D to Z is used in grading color.

(3) *Clarity:* the degree to which the diamond is free of "inclusions," i.e., internal or external marks. The test is conducted by shining a light through the stone. Clarity is also judged by a standard grading scale.

(4) *Cut:* the basic shape of the stone. There are five basic shapes, i.e., round, oval, square, pear, marquise. Since the round stone is the most popular for engagement rings, you should choose a round investment stone with 100 percent cutting of 58 facets in proper proportion.

Here are some helpful hints for investing in diamonds:

- Buy only diamonds with G.I.A. Certification . . . even if you have to pay for it.
- Deal with only reputable dealers who are financially capable of buying back the stone if necessary.
- Count on holding the stone for at least two years.
- Check prices with several brokers first and then cross-check their prices in the "Jeweler's Circular Keystone" magazine.

The DeBeers have done a great job of conditioning the mind of every teenage girl in the world to believe that a diamond is a girl's best friend. But few of those girls will ever realize that a ruby of comparable quality may be 50 times as rare.

Colored stones come mostly from small, family-owned mines which use spades and buckets as their only equipment. The price of colored stones is not determined by a cartel or syndicate but rather by true supply and demand factors. Up to 80 percent of a stone's value is determined by its color with the remaining value in the clarity and cut. The truer the color of red, blue, or green, the better the stone.

b. Rubies

Most rubies come from Thailand or Burma. Rubies have experienced tremendous price increases in the past five years. It is not unusual to pay $7,000 to $8,000 for a one-carat Burmese ruby. Recently at a Cristie's auction in Geneva, a woman paid $148,000 per carat (over $609,000) for a 4.12 carat pigeon's blood Burmese ruby.

c. Sapphires

Few people realize that sapphires and rubies come from the same mineral: corundum. If the corundum is red, it's a ruby; if it's blue (or pink or any other color), it's a sapphire. Therefore, it is no surprise that sapphires also come mostly from Thailand and Burma. In order to be an investment stone, a sapphire should be of at least a three-carat size. Sapphires have not demanded as high a price in recent history as rubies. No one seems to know why. But many dealers expect sapphires to make an upward move in the future.

d. Emeralds

The major sources for emeralds are Colombia, Africa, and Brazil. They, too, have experienced significant price increases in the past 10 years. But the demand for emeralds appears to have somewhat peaked out for the present time. It is possible that the less expensive tsavorite stone, a beautiful green gem from Tanzania, has stolen some of the emerald's market. But it is still not uncommon to pay $4,000 to $5,000 per carat for an emerald.

My personal opinion is that, even though I have owned gemstones in the past and presently do own some fine gemstones, I do not recommend them for the average portfolio. Gemstones, especially colored stones, are not easily liquidated. You can't just run right down and cash them out. Another problem is that you have a tendency to get personally attached to gemstones and forget that they are an investment to be traded or perhaps liquidated if the occasion arises.

6. COLLECTIBLES

Collectibles are things that *you* can appreciate while *they* appreciate. When the stock market began to sag in the 1960s, people began turning to collectibles. They started collecting every nostalgic item imaginable, from comic books to calliopes, from antique prints to airsick bags. The increasing inflation rates of the 1970s greatly encouraged this obsession.

Psychologically, I suppose, there is a security to be found in collecting and preserving a part of the stable past. But, moreover, I believe that at the grass roots level of society, people have been subconsciously trying to work out the gnawing economic reality that in times of inflation, you must convert your cash to something tangible in order to conserve its purchasing power.

Not all collectibles have stayed up with the rate of inflation. In fact, some silly collections may only be worth what the silly collector paid for them initially, thus proving to be an unworthy investment. However, many have spent the time to collect wisely and have made handsome profits from their investment. Some of the most popular collectibles are: stamps, rare books, oriental rugs, all kinds of antiques and rare art, and vintage autos.

But here are some drawbacks of collectibles:

- Most collectibles represent specialty markets; therefore, it requires a great deal of precious time to become an expert.
- Many collectibles fall in the category of a fad business.
- Many collectibles are perishable and are costly to maintain.
- Collectibles usually present a storage problem.
- There is a tendency to get emotionally attached to a collectible and hold on right past a good opportunity to sell.
- There may not be a ready market for your collectibles, therefore it should not be considered as a prime liquid investment.

B. Your Investment Strategy

Now that you have surveyed your various investment options, you need to begin to formulate a logical investment strategy that you can use as an everyday guide. While becoming familiar with the following diagram, keep in mind that you are planning to more effectively fulfill your stewardship or agency position as a *trustee* over everything that is now or ever will be in your Portfolio of Possessions. Remember, you do not own the possessions, but it *is* your responsibility to be a good manager so that your portfolio will multiply between now and when you give an accounting to the Master.

1. CENTER CIRCLE: **TITHE**

Notice that the tithe is at the hub or number-one circle of the diagram. A *minimum* of ten percent to 15 percent is to be included in this category. If this component is altered or rearranged, the whole wheel will become eccentric and out of balance.

I can't think of anything more exciting than taking the first portion of my earnings and investing them where they will pay eternal dividends forever and forever. I like to think of it as laying up treasures on the other side because that's where I'll abide forever.

YOUR INVESTMENT STRATEGY

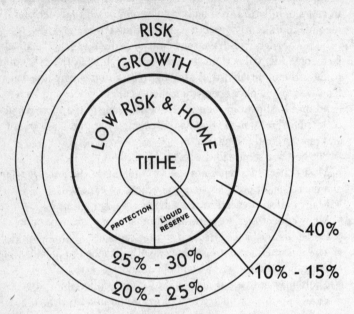

2. SECOND CIRCLE: **LOW RISK AND HOME**

You can call this your security circle. It will be essential to you and your family's well-being to pay special attention to this circle. Included in this circle are:

a. *Protection* (accident insurance, health insurance, life insurance, etc., that would be used upon the occurrence of a *physical catastrophe*).

b. *Liquid Reserve* (the readily available cash assets that would be used upon the occurrence of an *economic catastrophe*, i.e., loss of job, upset in the economy, etc.). I would recommend that an amount be set aside sufficient to cover your fixed expenses, i.e., house payment, car payment, basic utilities, etc., for a period of three to four months. That would give you time enough to cash out of some of your low-risk investment.

The amount of the *Liquid Reserve* category should not be held in cash but should be in something like a no-load money market fund where you would have access to it with just a telephone call or a telegram. "No load" simply means that you don't have to pay anything to set up the account, make deposits or withdrawals.

c. *Low Risk and Home* (your home and other low-risk investment areas). You probably were able to perceive from the earlier Investment Options section that I strongly recommend owning a home of your own if at all possible. Other investments that could be included in the Low-Risk Circle are Treasury bills, additional money market funds, certificates of deposit (CDs), and some types of tax-exempt municipal bonds. *It will pay you to get some local, personal advice at the time of your investing.*

Your Security Circle plus your Tithe Circle should total roughly 50 percent of your total investment package. Other than your home mortgage, this area should be pretty much debt free.

Notice now the *heavy ring around the outside of your Security Circle.* The dark ring is to graphically portray the concept that no matter what happens to the investments in the *Growth* area or the *Risk* area, they should never be able to penetrate and alter that which is inside the *Security Circle.*

You must live with the basic assumption that you might lose on investments in the *Growth* and *Risk* areas. But sustained losses in those areas must be kept separate from your *Security Circle.* For the well-being of yourself, your spouse, and your children, you must conscientiously adhere to this rule. Never invest in the Growth and Risk areas what you cannot afford to lose.

3. THIRD CIRCLE: **GROWTH**

Investments in your *Growth Circle* should account for approximately 25 percent to 30 percent of your total investment package. *You really have no business investing in this area or the Risk area if you have not been able to successfully manage the first two circles.*

Growth investments should include real estate, mutual funds, tax shelters with income and capital gains protection, e.g., oil and gas programs, bonds (rates "A" or better), your own business, limited partnerships, good rental property, solid growth stocks, etc.

A good rule of thumb for the Growth and Risk areas is to make sure that your personal liability does not extend to more than the individual investment itself. For example, in a real estate partnership make sure that you can lose no more than the amount that you put in. If the deal requires your accepting personal liability for the actions or investments of the other partners . . . pass up the deal. On a rental property, make sure that the loss of your equity is the extent of your liability. If you do not, you will allow a crack in the wall of your *Security Circle.*

4. FOURTH CIRCLE: **RISK**

Probably you will experience some of your most spectacular returns on your Risk investments. That's because big returns are usually commensurate with big risks.

In my experience and observation it would appear that most people adhere to an investment strategy that is diametrically opposed to sound business logic. If they get a little money ahead, they start investing in a pattern from the outside circle to the center, rather than from the inside to the outside. They do this with the destructive rationalization that if they can strike it rich from a high-risk investment . . . *then* they will have enough money to invest in the areas Growth, Protection, Liquidity, Tithe, etc. The only problem is that when they put all they own in the high-risk investment, plus sign for personal liability on things they do not have, they almost always lose. The results are devastating—upon themselves, their family relations, and God's kingdom.

Your Risk Circle could include mining stocks, precious gemstones, all types of collectibles, most stocks, gold and silver bullion, options and futures in the commodity market, exploration oil drilling, raw land, etc.

For certain, never accept extended personal liability in the Risk Circle. If there is to be a loss, let it be limited to the extent of an individual project. Your loss in a risk area should be affordable. No more than 20 percent to 25 percent of your assets should be included in the Risk Circle.

IV. YOUR OPPORTUNITIES

You have explored some interesting avenues whereby you can increase your earnings through prudent management. Those areas already discussed were Your Goals, Your Job, and Your Investments. But no exploration of how to earn all you can would be complete without devoting creative thought to YOUR OPPORTUNITIES.

A. Capitalize on Your Skills

Included in your *Portfolio of Possessions* may be some skills which, with very little effort, could be converted into increased earnings.

1. *Secretarial Services.* If you have a typewriter at home and would like to do some custom typing, it may take no more than a card on the bulletin board or an ad in a college newspaper to bring you plenty of "at home" work.
2. *Child Care Services.* With the increasing numbers of wives and mothers entering the full-time job market, there is a correlating increase in the demand for reliable child care.

3. *Sewing.* As the prices of ready-made garments continue to soar, your sewing skills will become more valuable. There has always been a demand for custom tailoring.
4. *Refinishing Furniture.* The crave for collectibles, especially antique furniture, has opened new doors of opportunity in this area.
5. *Auto Repairing.* During "tight money" times, people tend to have their cars repaired rather than replaced. A simple ad in the paper may bring you all the work you can handle.
6. *Carpet Service.* Most new homes are carpeted. But carpet doesn't stay new forever. Therefore, if your extra skills are in the areas of carpet laying or cleaning, you are right in style.
7. *Small Appliance Repairing.* The repair vs. replace advantage certainly applies when the economy tightens. There are many community colleges and vocational tech schools that offer classes where you could sharpen your repair skills.
8. *Radio* and *TV Industry.* Filmmaking, film editing, and script writing can be done easily in your home. Some disc jockeys are even prerecording their shows in their own private home studios for later airing.
9. *Journalism and Publishing.* Today there are demands for foreign language translation, proofreading, copywriting and editing, artwork and illustrations, technical writing, as well as the usual writing of articles for religious and secular magazines, books, and newsletters. These skills can be marketed in your "spare time."
10. *Advertising.* Literally thousands of small advertising agencies across the country are today being operated out of homes.
11. *Educational Services.* Additional money is being earned today in tutoring of remedial reading and math, speech therapy, vocational counseling, art instruction, music lessons, and correcting test papers for all levels of education.

B. Capitalize on Your Hobbies

In addition to your skills, you may have some hobbies that could very easily start earning you income.
1. *Photography.* In addition to the more traditional photo taking for weddings, baby dedications, etc., why not start a service where you go into people's homes, photograph and write a detailed description of their valuable household items and antiques for insurance purposes?
2. *Gardening.* People in your neighborhood still love fresh produce. Make your gardening pay off. If you like to raise flowers, then try selling them to nearby restaurants, offices, hotels, etc. Or you

could start a service of leasing and caring for green plants in reception areas and offices of businesses near you.

3. *Doll House Miniatures.* Recently I spoke at a Christian Women's Club luncheon where they featured a woman and her husband who were making a very profitable business out of their hobby of building miniatures.

V. YOUR OPTION TO BARTER

A. What Is Barter?

Barter is simply trading *what'cha have* for *what'cha want.* Barter is the most natural form of order. You have been trading since you were born. You traded for all your acquired possessions.

But somewhere in our economy we became addictively oriented to "money." The addiction came about because of the *presumed convenience* of using a money system. It appeared to be simpler to pay money to a plumber to come and fix the bathroom drainpipe than to find a plumber in the neighborhood who would perform the repair job with the agreement that there would be a reciprocal compensation of carpentry work, mechanical work on his truck, fresh produce from the garden, music lessons for his kids, or color photos of the family for next year's Christmas cards.

But, historically, during times of *economic depression, inflation,* or *abusive taxation,* the barter system has always revived, outweighing the convenience of the regular money system. The more worthless money becomes, the more likely it is that commodities will become "money."

But why is a section on barter included in the chapter "Earn All You Can"? The answer is, if you can barter for things that would normally require cash, then you will not have had to spend that cash. Unspent cash is the same as earning more money!

It is not at all unreasonable to believe that you could trade for gasoline, batteries, tires, a car or truck lease, car pooling, fresh produce, dairy products, butchered beef, frozen foods, your clothing, clothing for the kids, baby-sitting, landscaping, painting, house repairs, car repairs, etc., all of which you otherwise would have paid cash for during the month.

Bartering is really the only logical way to beat inflation. You look beyond the price of things and begin to deal with relative values. After having gone through the chapter on the *Economy,* you can understand the concept that, *inflation as we know it today would be impossible in the barter system.* That is because it takes the governmental manipulation of the money system in order to have a sustained increase in all prices, i.e., inflation.

B. How to Use Barter

I have discovered that most people are subconsciously good traders. That is, without doubt, due to the fact that we all used barter exclusively until the day we learned to use cash. Most likely, you have reverted back to using barter upon occasion without even being aware of it. For example, you may have watched the neighbor's kids while the neighbor picked up something for you at the store, or shoveled the snow from the widow's sidewalks next door in exchange for some homemade pies or freshly baked bread. Politicians even use a primitive form of bartering when they lobby or the passing of a favorite piece of legislature. It's called favor trading or vote trading.

So let's see if we can develop a procedure that will make it easier to *attempt* bartering. List the following in your notebook:

1. *Determine what'cha have available for trade.* Many times you may find something you need that belongs to someone who is willing to trade with you. Then, he asks, "What do you have that you will trade me for it?" You answer, "I don't know," and that ends the negotiation. You must have your inventory well in mind. Your list will be divided into two parts, i.e., *services* and *things*.
2. *Determine what'cha want.* This list will again be divided into two parts, i.e., *services* and *things*. When you discover that you want or need something, write it down on one of the lists.
3. *Find someone with whom to trade.* To barter you must find the person who has what you want and will exchange for what you have. Not only is this easier than what you expected, but it's a lot of fun. It becomes a challenging game to match up what you need with what someone else has. Two of the simplest places to find what you need are grocery store bulletin boards and newspaper classified ads.

These are great sources, because people who go to the trouble of placing a card on a bulletin board or pay money to run a newspaper ad are definitely telling you that they have something they don't want. "Don't wants" are the easiest things in the world for which to trade. We call "don't wants" "white elephants," and they come in every shape and size possible, from an antique car that is taking up too much space in the family garage (and the wife has said, "Either that car goes or I go"), to the apartment complex that is having management problems. Someone's "white elephant" may be just the vehicle you need for your next *economic safari*.

Another way to find barter partners is by word of mouth. You may even have to become more friendly with those around you than you are today. Be willing to talk about what you have and what you are looking for. Today many neighborhoods are organizing little local bartering groups. I would recommend that these groups be kept to around 20 to 30 people. They meet once a month at someone's house and take turns presenting their lists of what they have and what they need. This is a great educational process for the whole family.

4. *Consummate the trade.* The first couple of times you attempt to barter, it may seem a little awkward. But the anxiety quickly goes away with a little practice.

Do barter deals really work? Yes, when both sides benefit from the trade. You may have to ask several people in order to find the one who feels that he will also benefit from the exchange. But again, usually the reason we don't barter is because we are too timid to ask.

The story is told about the little boy who was standing out beside his curbside sign trying to sell his puppy. The sign states: "Puppy for sale, $10,000."

A man, on his way to work that morning, chuckled as he passed the little boy. Not seeing the sign, the puppy, or the little boy on his way home, the man decided to stop and see if the little boy had successfully made his sale.

"Did you sell your puppy today?"

"Sure did!"

"Did you get your $10,000 for it?"

"Sure did!"

"My goodness, how did you do it?"

"Well, I worked a trade!"

"What did you trade for?"

"Two $5,000 kittens!"

Here are some helpful hints for bartering:

- Be sure to utilize your "What'cha Have" and "What'cha Want" lists. Know specifically what you are looking for and determine in you own mind the value of what you have.
- Don't be afraid to ask to barter. You are not only benefiting yourself, but you are also benefiting the person with whom you are trading.
- Be enthusiastic in your bartering but never overanxious or overbearing.
- Ask lots of questions and be genuinely interested in the other person's article or service.
- Bartering in person is 100 times more effective than trying to barter over the phone.
- Keep your present cash flow coming in from your job, etc. Work into the barter system gradually.

- It is not necessary to discuss "price" during a trade. Just stick to dealing with the items to be traded.
- Never be derogatory about the item another person has to trade. Either you can use it or you cannot.
- Give the other person a better deal than he has coming. That way you will have him coming back later for another trade.
- Don't make irrational offers, e.g., a broken lawn mower for a diamond ring. You will only lose your credibility.
- You may "sweeten" the deal with a little bit of cash added to your trade or offer to pay the electrician for his wire and switch boxes if he will trade out his labor.
- Make sure everyone is happy with the trade. Never try to shove a deal together; it will only bring repercussions later. It's better to walk away from a deal than to put up with "trader's remorse" later. Just remember that there are lots of people out there who will be eager to trade with you.
- Don't be afraid to take something on trade that you, yourself, will not use. You can throw it in on the next transaction. Build a spendable inventory of goods and services.
- If you make a deal, live with it.
- Keep an ongoing list of names and phone numbers of people who are inclined to barter. Make contact with them periodically and let them know "What'cha Have" and "What'cha Want."

If you operate your own business, you have a great opportunity to practice barter. People will many times come to you to trade for your product. You can apply the same principles that we have previously discussed.

C. Barter and Taxes

One of the nicest things about barter is that no "money" changes hands. Individuals are not the only ones who have become addictively oriented to cash; so have governments. They don't really understand barter either. Therefore, their tax collection systems are set up to deal with cash. If you are an amateur making "in kind" trades with neighbors and relatives, it is more than likely that you will not have a taxable situation. But the barter of professional services, i.e., bookkeeping in exchange for meals at a restaurant, etc., is considered taxable income by the Internal Revenue Service, and fair market value must be declared.

The Internal Revenue Service code includes the Common Notable Exchange Clause 1031(a):

No gain or loss shall be recognized if property held for productive use in trade or business or for investment is exchanged solely for property of a like kind to be held either for productive use in trade or business or for investment.

However, once you "cash out" of the investment, you must pay capital gains tax.

Historically, IRS has not concerned itself with convenience bartering, e.g., one farmer helping another farmer build his barn in exchange for his help in planting the spring wheat crop, or the housewife exchanging baby-sitting for custom sewing. But if you are a member of a formal barter club or use the services of a barter broker, there really is no way to escape the impact of the income tax.

If you get into bartering seriously, then I would recommend you rely heavily on the services and advice of a competent attorney or accountant who is familiar with bartering—and be sure to trade for his services.

D. Barter and Kingdom Business

If you have let your creativity run rampant while working through this last section, you no doubt have realized that there are opportunities to barter on *every level* of the economy. In fact, every relationship, economic or personal, can be enhanced once you learn the fine art of bartering. Bartering will allow *needs to be met* in the most creative method. The principles of barter are the same whether you are applying them to a small, simple deal or a very complex and sophisticated trade. You will probably discover that, once you start bartering, it is as easy to put together a big deal as it is a small one.

Once you begin to utilize the art of bartering, remember, skill must also be accounted for in your Portfolio of Possessions under the section, "MY TALENTS AND SPECIAL ABILITIES." What an exciting thought! You have the opportunity to develop the skill of bartering and then dedicate that new ability to God for the advancement of Kingdom business.

It is possible for you today to take something you have and trade it for something that could be used in Kingdom business. For example, right now my brother Bill is in the negotiation stage of trading some of his assets for $750,000 worth of medical equipment that would be used in many missionary outposts around the world. He recognizes it as his stewardship responsibility to see if he can consummate the trade. What a thrill!

You may not have $750,000 in assets that you could trade, but you have *something* in your Portfolio of Possessions. Look around: what is needed in your local area of Kingdom business? Maybe it's a new lawn mower for the church. Maybe a new Sunday School bus, or perhaps the old one needs a new paint job. How about a new sign in front of your sanctuary, or a new roof, or some pretty shrubs? What do you have that you could use for barter to obtain those needs?

But maybe what you really need is going to cost a lot more than you have right now. Let's suppose what is really needed is a new gymnasium and Sunday School classroom building. Or—suppose you really needed the large free and clear piece of vacant land next to the church for additional parking. Is it possible to barter for something like that? Yes, it may take you several steps of "trading up" to accomplish it, but it can be done.

One of the little known but beautiful features of "trading up" for Kingdom business is that the *government has made provision for such transactions.* When you are trading up on any "like kind" of barter, the government allows a postponement of the tax consequences. This is because there is the presumption that someday you will "cash out" in some type of a sale; and when you "cash out," you will then subtract the original base in the first property from the sales price of the last property and pay your tax consequence on the difference, i.e., you profit. But if you give your final property to a qualified charitable organization, you realized *no taxable gain* on the entire transaction even though you had the advantage of the leverage factor throughout the sequence of trades. Obviously, you cannot take a contribution receipt for more than your base . . . *but who cares?* You are able to *transfer your total accumulated equity into Kingdom business without tax consequence.* If you do not utilize the barter system, your gift will be *substantially* smaller.

7
Save All You Can

INTRODUCTION

Living off next week's paycheck has become a way of life for millions of American consumers. The price of an object is given little consideration so long as the monthly installment payments aren't too steep. Groceries are purchased on a daily basis dependent upon what sounds good for that day's menu. There is a subtle persuasion to spend anything found in the wallet or purse because tomorrow the prices are going to increase.

MUTT & JEFF © 1974 A Edita S. deBeaumont.

In a crazy world like this, how can you save any money? Even the government recognizes that people can't save their money. That is why taxes are deducted weekly from their paychecks, whether they like it or not, on an automatic basis. The government knows that the average taxpayer would never apply enough discipline to set aside money for taxes and pay them all at once on April 15.

Most people believe that living expenses will use up *all of their income* so that there will never be enough left over to save. And guess what! Those who believe that are *always right*. They never have enough left over to save. Changing your economic habit patterns is sometimes as much a spiritual decision as a psychological or financial one. Solomon declared, "The wise man saves for the future, but the foolish man spends whatever he gets (Prov. 21:20, TLB).

This chapter on "Save All You Can" is not for just reading. You are going to have to work through its three parts:

   I. THE NEED FOR SAVING
  II. A METHOD FOR SAVING
 III. SIMPLE SUGGESTIONS FOR SAVING

I. THE NEED FOR SAVING

A. Savings: The Source of Investment Capital

In the previous chapter you were presented the idea of "Your Investment Strategy" . . . with all of its different circles. The most common response, especially from the young married couples, has been, "We are having a tough enough time trying to meet the needs of the Security Circle . . . to say nothing of having enough to *ever invest beyond that*. Would someone just please help us figure out how to save enough to get the pressure off?"

I have a real empathy for couples who are having financial pressures. In fact, the motivation for this book grew in part out of observing the financial practices of nearly 200 young married kids who were in a Sunday School Annie and I taught. Most of them were living from one paycheck to another, always about 64 hours away from bankruptcy. They were experiencing firsthand that money pressures could result in physical illnesses, spoiled relationships with their friends, unpleasant experiences with their parents and families, and bitter quarrels between themselves. They also discovered that financial pressures even have a way of taking the keen edge off their spiritual condition. Most of them had a tough time realizing that *it's not so much the quantity of money you have . . . but how you spend it that makes the difference.* Many of them were already earning salaries that were in excess of any of their early dreams.

However, if you want more money to apply to your investment strategy, you will find that systematic savings are *the source* of investment capital. There will never be a convenient time to save. The wife will be pregnant, the kids will be sick, the car will need repairs, etc. But with discipline and intelligent planning, it is possible to become a better steward . . . and even enjoy the process.

I am convinced that you have to *learn* how to successfully handle money through instruction and experience. Having earned and spent money all your adult life doesn't make you any more capable of successfully handling it than watching Sunday afternoon football makes you a pro quarterback! You must be willing to personally learn and experience the rules and disciplines of the game. That is especially true when it comes to saving money.

By the time I as 14 I was in charge of all the window displays for our local Montgomery Ward. I recall that I was super careful to get the women's ready-to-wear windows done early in the week. If I waited and tried to do them on Saturday, there would be outside the window a crowd of about 25 migrant farm workers who had just been brought to town from the area farms. They would get off the bus and stand and point their fingers, nudge each other, and laugh like crazy at the young kid in the window trying to dress all those naked mannequins. A cheap thrill . . . at my expense! But, I also remember that when payday rolled around, all the employees would wait in line to receive our little yellow envelopes. Inside those envelopes would be *cash*. (They actually paid us in *CASH!*) I would open the envelope, make sure it contained the right amount of money, and then head for home. At home I had a line of chipped A & W Root Beer mugs on top of my dresser. I used to play a little game: I would see if I could move my money from the mug on the right end of the dresser to the mug on the left end. The mug on the right was for coins; the mug on the left was for crisp $100 bills. Whenever I had enough coins to make a dollar, I would exchange it for a paper dollar. When I had five $1.00 bills, I would exchange them for a $5.00 bill and move it up one mug. As I accumulated the money, I would move it from the $5.00 mug to the $10.00 mug . . . to the $20.00 mug . . . to the $50.00 mug . . . and finally to the $100.00 mug. I don't recall anyone ever telling me that I ought to do that . . . I just did it. I also remember that there was another mug. But I kept that mug in the top dresser drawer. It was my "tithe mug." My thinking was that if someone was going to steal my mugs, they could take the ones on top of the dresser. But, for sure, I didn't want anyone to take my "tithe mug." That was for the Lord! I learned many things from that experience.

I learned that there were some real benefits to saving. First, there was a real sense of tangible satisfaction, a sense of security. If I wanted to take a girl out on a date, I didn't have to ask Mom and Dad for the money. I bought my own clothes, paid my own tuition to a private school, etc. Second, I learned that I could receive a *return on my savings*. I always had cash on hand to take advantage of a bargain. I found that I could also loan out some of my money and be paid back with interest. Having cash available even made trades go together easier. If I could dump in just a little cash, the motivation for trading would suddenly increase. I later found out that institutions like banks and savings companies would pay to use my money . . . just like in the days of "Gaffney Goldsmith." I was finding out that indeed, *systematic savings are the source of investment capital.*

B. Two Concepts of Savings in One

As I have grown a little older, I have discovered something else about savings. It means different things to different people. To one person it may mean an account in a local savings and loan paying 5 1/4 percent. Mention savings to another, and it may spark a picture in his mind of the coffee can filled with gemstones and gold Krugerrands buried in his backyard. To another, savings may mean driving across town to the self-service truck stop to save three cents a gallon on gasoline. Someone else may equate savings with turning down thermostats and shutting off light switches. But all those different ideas can be divided into *two* basic concepts of savings: *prevention of waste* and *preservation on deposit.*

1. PREVENTION OF WASTE

The key word here is "frugal," i.e., being prudent in your spending. If you eliminate unnecessary expenditures, you automatically increase the available funds for discretionary spending. That is done without increasing a single penny of new income.

If you need more to spend on those necessary items within the Security Circle of Your Investment Strategy, perhaps you should consider spending less on the goods and services that you are presently purchasing. *Many times it is easier and more effective to be frugal than it is to earn more money.*

You have often heard that "a penny saved is a penny earned." No longer is that necessarily true. Today, *a penny saved is two pennies earned!* If you are married and file a joint return with the IRS reporting $40,000 taxable income, you pay $380 of the next $1,000 income in federal tax. In other words, "Welcome to the 38 percent tax bracket!" Doesn't that make you want to go right out and earn another $1,000? And, to make things more interesting, that does not include the six percent or eight percent that might be owed on Social Security. What can you do about it? You can begin to *save* more as an alternative to earning more. For example, if you were planning to eat out at a restaurant where you would spend $40.00 with tip, but you decided to eat at home and spend $10.00, you would have saved $30.00; i.e., you would have $30.00 more in your bank account that you otherwise would not have had. To go out and earn that extra $30.00 to put into your bank account, you would really have had to earn $48.38, i.e., $30.00 for you and $18.80 for the tax man.

Instead of driving all the way across the country to spend your traditional two-week vacation at the resort, suppose you used a little creativity. Suppose you found a "fun place" closer to home that could be used to create the same number of wonderful memories. Instead of paying perhaps $1,500, you might have to pay only $500: a savings of $1,000 in your account.

Study carefully the following chart which emphasizes the importance of being careful in your spending. The chart shows how much money you would have to have in a savings account at 5 3/4 percent for its interest payments to equal the same after-tax return if you would have simply been careful in your shopping, driving, etc., and would have saved $250, $50, $750, $1,000, or $1,500.

'IT PAYS TO BE FRUGAL'

	Amount Saved by Being Frugal	$250	$500	$750	$1,000	$1,500
	Amount needed on deposit @ 5¾% to equal same yield after tax					
YOUR TAX BRACKET 10%		$ 4,831	$ 9,662	$14,493	$19,324	$28,985
20%		$ 5,435	$10,870	$16,304	$21,739	$32,609
30%		$ 6,211	$12,422	$18,633	$24,845	$37,267
40%		$ 7,246	$14,493	$21,739	$28,985	$43,478
50%		$ 8,696	$17,391	$26,087	$34,783	$52,174
60%		$10,870	$21,739	$32,609	$43,478	$65,217

EXPLANATION: Find the amount you saved by being frugal in your spending; then find your personal tax bracket; find at the intersection of those two the amount that you would need to have on deposit, earning 5¾% interest, to give you the same annual after-tax yield.

2. PRESERVATION ON DEPOSIT

In addition to preventing waste, you must begin to systematically put money into a reserve. After you have paid your tithe on your paycheck, the *next ten percent* should be set aside in savings to be applied toward the next step in Your Investment Strategy. If you don't take your savings from the top, you can be certain that it will not be found at the bottom. Don't go overboard and try to save 30 percent or 40 percent of your regular paycheck. Be reasonable and stick with a consistent ten percent. It is more important that you are *consistent* than extravagant.

You will have to create a savings habit built on consistent repetition. If you really have difficulty disciplining yourself, you might consider having your employer automatically deposit a portion of your paycheck directly into your credit union. Or you could authorize your bank to make an automatic transfer from your checking account to your savings account after each payday or once a month. You will then start becoming aware of your financial situation and realize how relatively simple it is to get it under control and keep it that way.

Another good way to save is by depositing all refund or reimbursement checks into an account before you are tempted to cash them and let them get away from you. Try to put *at least* half of your income tax refund directly into savings. Also, you should *at least* split any pay raises or bonuses with half going into savings. Or, when you have finished paying off an installment loan, e.g., car loan, keep making the payment, since you are used to doing it anyway. Only now make the payment into your savings account. Those methods make it quite easy to save since you have not grown accustomed to having those amounts to spend on a regular basis.

It is quite possible that getting into a habit of saving on a regular basis will be one of the toughest assignments you have ever undertaken. But, no one has ever attained financial success without getting his saving/spending behavior under control. What you deposit into a savings account or credit union should probably not stay there for very long, at least in today's market. If you will recall what was said in Chapter Five on determining the *Real Rate of Interest,* you will quickly recognize the importance of not leaving your savings in a traditional savings account for an extended period of time. Remember that the *real* rate of interest is the interest being paid on your savings minus the rate of inflation.

So, if you are receiving eight percent interest on your savings and the rate of inflation is five percent, then your *Real Rate of Interest* being earned is three percent. You can quickly see that at a low rate of interest paid during the time of high inflation, it is possible to *lose* money by keeping it in such an account. For example, if you were receiving only 5 1/4 percent interest and the inflation rate was six percent, you would be *losing* three quarters of a percent for the privilege of *letting them* use your money! It is recommended that you immediately begin applying the funds to the appropriate circle of Your Investment Strategy. Certainly, it would not be wise to leave any funds idle! *Hoarding* is foolish as well as unscriptural.

When looking for a savings institution for your deposits, you will be wise to consider the following factors:

1. How often is interest compounded?
2. What is the method of calculating interest?
3. What is the rate of interest?

Make sure it's daily interest figured from day of deposit to day of withdrawal.

There is a little rule of thumb that will be beneficial to you in your savings planning. It is called the "Rule of 70/72." If you want to calculate how long it takes your money *to double* at a compounded rate of return, simply divide the percentage rate being paid: e.g., nine, if it's nine percent into "70" or "72" (whichever number the return divides into exactly) and get the number of years. For example, nine would divide exactly into 72, eight times. So it would take you *eight years* to *double your money* at *nine percent return.* If your return was ten percent, ten would divide into 70 exactly seven times. So it would take you *seven years* to *double your money* at *ten percent.*

II. A METHOD FOR SAVING

A. You Need a Map, Sonny!

I recall how frustrated I was when we first moved to Denver. The locations of the downtown streets were dictated by the South Platte River and Cherry Creek. That seemed only right since they had gotten there first. But it made it difficult to find certain places. I would ask for directions to one of the downtown buildings and invariably have to stop somewhere along the way for some reinforcing guidance. The building would somehow never be where it was supposed to be! One day a kind gentleman solved my problem: "I'll give you some *real good directions.* What you need is a *map,* Sonny!"

He was absolutely right! I got a map, and I soon discovered that even though the streets were not "square with the world," those majestic Rocky Mountains would never move around. They were always on the *west.* Knowing *that,* I could use my *map* to get me anywhere I needed to go.

But what kind of a map could be used as a method for saving? I'm certainly glad you asked, because I have come up with another acrostic for easy remembering:

Your Financial Map

M MONEY
A ACCOUNTABILITY
P PROGRAM

I am thoroughly convinced that people become good stewards and stay good stewards by *being willing* to keep tight control over their finances. Just "more money" will not solve a financial situation that is not under control. But a method that is designed to give financial structure and guidance will do much to reduce strife and hassle within a family.

Your MAP must be *realistic* and then followed to *reality*. It should become a lifetime approach to controlling your finances. The difficulty of following your MAP the first year or two will be rewarded greatly in later years.

You should make the MAP work for you; it should be your servant. *It should suggest to you* what kind of house you can live in, what kind of car you can drive, what kind and how many clothes you can hang in your closet. Look at your MAP as something that is devoted to keeping you from embarrassment and wasted energy.

A fellow told me just recently, "A financial plan is an insult to me because it implies that I can't earn enough to live and spend the way I want." The sad truth is that he *has been insulted* in the past *and will be again* in the future . . . not by a financial accountability plan, but by the lack thereof. Christ's admonition throughout the New Testament is for you to have a plan of action. You are to sit down, count the cost, know where you are headed, and how your are going to get there. (See Lk. 14:28-31.) In may cases even worry and fret are eliminated when a good plan of action is implemented. *Your financial MAP offered herein is designed to give you a simple program for money accountability.* It really is more than just a plan or a blueprint; it's a *program* that will necessitate your involvement. A *blueprint* may be nice, but you need to go ahead and build your *house.* When the cold storms of financial adversity hit, you will need more than just a plan or blueprint to keep you safe and warm. You will need a *refuge.*

B. Your MAP in 3D

The only thing better than having a map would be if the map were in 3D! So, consider now the 3Ds that will give your MAP more clarity.
1. **DEVELOP** Efficient Records for MAP
2. **DIVIDE** Responsibilities of MAP
3. **DETERMINE** Details of MAP

1. DEVELOP EFFICIENT RECORDS FOR MAP

The overall success of your MAP will depend to a large degree upon careful record keeping. The system should be simple . . . the simpler the better! I personally can't handle an overabundance of details, so I promise that our MAP has been designed with simplicity in mind!

a. Locate and Organize Personal Documents

If we are going to do this thing right, we might as well start at the beginning! If you needed an important document, could you find it within 60 seconds? Do you have all of your credit card numbers recorded in one list? How about all insurance policies, savings account numbers, safe-deposit box numbers, investments, bonds, stocks, car titles, mortgage, retirement records and fund account numbers, wills, income tax records, etc.? Take as many pages as are necessary in your notebook to list *every* important document number, location, agent's name and address, and any other essential information.

For Better or For Worse   **by Lynn Johnston**

Copyright, 1981, Universal Press Syndicate. Reprinted with permission. All rights reserved.

b. Develop a System for Monthly Record Keeping

Every month you are faced with incoming statements, checkbooks that have to be reconciled, checks that have to be written, etc. When under control, those functions can become very mechanical—but when out of control, count on a high degree of frustration that could be eliminated by developing a simple system.

- *First, acquire a financial folder* . . . one with pockets in it. Place into the folder all current bills, payment books, current bank statements and canceled checks, sales slips and charge card receipts for the month, a checkbook, blank envelopes and stamps, and a small pocket calculator.
- *Next, pick a specific day* of the month, shortly after you receive your bank statement. *Reconcile your bank statement and pay the bills on that date.* A couple of hours one day per month will usually be enough to take care of your monthly money transactions. When bills come in after your bill-paying date, unless it is an emergency, simply put them in the financial folder until next month. Keep the system under control. Keep it simple! There is no reason for you to be intimidated by the mechanics of handling money.

After you have written the checks, put the sales slips and receipts into an envelope marked with the month and year and put them in the same drawer with your bank statements. That should clean out your financial folder, and you will be ready for next month. There are some definite advantages to having all your monthly financial matters in one concise, portable location.

2. DIVIDE RESPONSIBILITIES OF MAP

For households that include two adult members, it is absolutely imperative that both know and understand the state of the family finances. Miserly behavior as well as spendthrift behavior tends to vanish when there is financial unity. But it will usually fall the responsibility of one person to be the bookkeeper. The designee for bookkeeper is usually quite easily recognized. It is the one . . .

- Who enjoys organization and detail.
- Whose aptitude includes working with numbers.
- Who is most oriented to specific dates and obligations.
- Whose schedule would best allow the bookkeeping responsibilities.

In order for your MONEY ACCOUNTABILITY PROGRAM (MAP) to work successfully, both parties must be satisfied with their responsibilities. If you don't like the responsibility assignments, change them!

3. DETERMINE THE DETAILS OF MAP

The real key to a sound Money Accountability Program is grasping clearly the concept behind the receipts and disbursements so that you *know* where your money goes. The more accurate your information, the better control you will have over your money. In order to gain that accurate information, there are several details to determine.

a. Determine Cash Flow

First of all, you must determine how much money you have each month to spend. Fortunately for you, all you will have to do is transfer numbers from your notebook where you already figured out your take-home pay. Withheld taxes are ignored at this point. However, it should be clarified here: Don't allow more to be withheld for deductions than is accurate. Some people report fewer dependents so their employer will withhold more in taxes, thereby giving them more of a tax refund at the end of the year. That really doesn't make sense. The government has your money all that time and pays you zero percent on it. You are not even thanked for being noble. Take that money as part of your savings and invest it in the "Security Circle" of *Your Investment Strategy*.

b. Determine Expenses

Expenses are divided into two categories: *fixed*—those over which you have little immediate control, and *flexible*—those over which you have control on a periodic basis.

In order to more accurately determine your expenses, it is

129

recommended that *you and your spouse keep close records of spending for 30 or 60 days*. The easiest way that I know to do that is to write checks for *everything* for that period of time . . . that's right *everything*. You will then have a permanent record which you can analyze to determine your fixed and flexible expenses. The other alternative is for both husband and wife to carry a slip of paper for the 30 or 60 days upon which they can enter *every transaction*, right down to the "last thin dime."

(1) *Fixed Expenses*

Your fixed expenses are those payments you must pay because of contracts or previous agreements, i.e., rent or mortgage payment, insurance, bank loan, etc. You may have fixed payments that occur only two, three, or four times a year, e.g., insurance premiums, tuition, car license, etc. Take the total yearly amount due for each item and divide it by 12 to get the monthly amount you need to put aside to meet those payments. Take a page in your notebook and list all your fixed expenses with their average monthly amount. Begin your fixed expense list with tithe and then savings of ten percent. In a column beside those amounts enter an "adjusted expense" amount indicating any expenses that can be cut back somewhat. At the bottom identify the totals for both columns.

(2) *Flexible Expenses*

Some expenses are called "flexible" because they can be *bent* . . . until *you* are *broke*. Perhaps the greatest threat to your MAP is compulsive buying. It's easy to get into trouble with flexible expenses, but *you* have the right to adjust and control them. They include food, vacations, personal items, subscriptions, entertainment, clothing, gasoline, etc.

Title another page in your notebook, "Flexible Expenses." Leave a blank margin down the left hand side before each item is listed. Then to the right of the items allow *three* columns for entering figures. Title one column, "Actual Monthly Expenses," another "Ideal Monthly Expenses," and the third column "Adjusted Expenses."

At this point fill in only the "Actual Monthly Expenses" (as calculated from your 30 to 60 day records) and the "Ideal Monthly Expenses."

Remember, items that have annual, semiannual, or quarterly payments, e.g., magazine subscriptions, professional dues, etc., are to be figured on an annual basis, then divided by 12 to find the monthly obligation. There should be a category and an average amount on one of these two pages for *everything* you've spent money on over the last year.

Now, total your two columns on your Flexible Expense page.

c. Determine the Difference Between Income and Expenses

Well, are you overspending, underspending, or breaking even? Use the following exercise to find out.

INCOME versus EXPENSES

Total Monthly Income: $ _____ *(a)*
(take from last line of *"Take-Home Pay"* work sheet

Total Monthly Expenses: $ _____ *(b)*
(add totals from *"Fixed Expenses"* work sheet and *"Flexible Expenses"* work sheet

Difference between *Income* and *Expenses*: $ _____ *(c)*
(subtract *b* from *a*)

How did you fare?

- If line *(c)* shows a *plus figure*, you are to be congratulated: You are living within your income. It should be relatively easy now to proceed and discover some fun ways of pulling some more dollars out that can accompany your savings and be applied toward *Your Investment Strategy*. Keep up the good work!
- If line *(c)* is a *zero*, you are just breaking even. You, too, are to be congratulated, however, because your MAP has just included ten percent off the top for savings. Please accept the challenge now to press on and find some new ways to save.
- If line *(c)* is a *minus figure*, it is probably not news to you that you are spending more than you are bringing home. Adhering to your MAP can change all of that. I have yet to see any couple who cannot live within 80 percent of their income if they are willing to alter their life-style. Usually, the problem is with the "willingness" level. Remember, your MAP should never for a moment be considered a punishment to you or your spouse, but rather a method that will get you from where you are to where you want to be. The MAP is your friend.

d. Determine Priorities

Marketing institutions have one goal in mind: *Influence the priority system of the consumer so that person purchases the desired product.*

Advertising campaigns are almost exclusively aimed at the *emotional influence* rather than the *intellectual.* They appeal to the emotions of fear, prestige, greed, or sex. They count on people spending their money on what they have been programmed to *want* . . . which is not necessarily what they *need.* Therefore, one of the most valid exercises which you can perform is to consciously review your spending behavior and see if you are purchasing the goods and services that you really need.

Such an exercise is sometimes difficult to perform because it's tough to determine what is *most important* to you. But if you can force yourself to crystalize your priorities, you are well on your way to making your MAP a success.

Gaining control of your Flexible Expenses first, and then working on your Fixed Expenses, is usually the most successful step-by-step approach to a financial program. In preparation for this exercise, I would like for you to do two things:

1. Go back and review your crystalized *goals* from Chapter Five.
2. Ask the Holy Spirit to help you with your value system.

Now, look again at your Flexible Expense work sheet. Go down through each time and assign a value of one, two, or three in the left-hand margin according to its level of importance to you. *For a married couple, it is mandatory for the exercise to be performed by both husband and wife.* It is quite likely that you will discover some interesting details about each other as you go through the list.

Place a one next to those items which are *most important to you.*

No matter how logical or illogical your priority might appear to someone else, you have the right to it, just as long as you are willing to adjust and perhaps even severely cut back spending in some other area in order to make up for it.

Next place a two by the items which *are important* to you; and upon which you would like to spend money—but they are *not as important as those in category one.* For example, you might like to take the family to brunch after church on Sunday morning. Occasionally, you might even eat with others from your church, and you consider that an important time of personal contact and fellowship. Or the wife may consider it important to call long distance to her mother once a week to check up on how she's doing.

Next, place a three on all the remaining items. Of course, the items in three are *important* . . . in fact, crucial. But they *may not hold high significance beyond their actual need.* For example, magazine subscriptions or even your car or food. You know you have to have a car to get you around, but it is not of such high importance that it be the newest or slickest. Likewise, with food, you obviously have to eat, but not the latest fad food or fancy specialty.

Make sure each item is assigned a one, two, or three.

e. Decide on Cuts

Now that you have determined your priorities, you can take an effective and intelligent approach toward making some spending cuts. *Your objective will be to make line (c) from your Income versus Expenses work sheet come out to a plus number . . . or at least a zero.*

You have one blank column remaining on the extreme right side of your Flexible Expenses work sheet entitled "Adjusted Expense."

Go through all of the items on the number three category. *Reduce each "Actual Expense" amount by one third and enter the new figure in the "Adjusted Expense" column.* For example, if your "Actual Expense" for *dry cleaning* had been $25.00, you will now enter $17.00 ($25.00 X 66.6% = $16.66) in the "Adjusted Expense" column. Continue this approach for all items in the number three category. Now add up all your new totals of *Fixed Expenses* and *Flexible Expenses* and see if line (c) of your Income Flow versus Expenses comes out to a plus or at least a zero number.

If not, continue similarly to the items in the number-two category.

If it is necessary to reduce amounts from your number-one category, it is better to use your imagination and ingenuity than to set an arbitrary percentage for reduction. After all, you have decided those are the *most important* things to you.

If at this point your cutbacks have still not brought line (c) of your *Income versus Expenses* to a plus or at least a zero number, you will need to then consider your *Fixed Expenses.* Occasionally, it will be easier to adjust a fixed expenditure than to tamper with an item in the number-one category of your flexible spending. For example, one of your fixed expenses may be a monthly installment payment on your motor home, camper, or snowmobiles. You may decide that the simplest way to bring you MAP into proper focus is to sell the item. In *extreme* cases, it might even be necessary to eliminate a devastating house payment by moving into a less expensive place to live.

In all of your cutback maneuvers, do not be tempted to reduce the amounts of your tithe or savings. I am convinced that God will help you find creative alternatives in being frugal.

f. Develop a Monthly MAP

Once you have your *Income versus Expenses* work sheet under control, you are ready to set up your short-range Monthly MAP. You do that by simply transferring the amounts from your "Adjusted Expense" columns of your Fixed Expenses and Flexible Expenses work sheets to your Monthly MAP. Those "Adjusted Expenses" will now be entered in the column entitled "Projected Expenses." The other column of your Monthly MAP is your "Actual Expenses," i.e., what you really paid that month for the specific item. Please notice at the bottom of your Monthly MAP you will find space for you to total your "Actual Expenses" which are to be subtracted from your monthly take-home pay. You should take the "plus" difference and apply toward the appropriate circle of Your Investment Strategy.

Of course, you will have to make periodic evaluations and adjustments of your MAP, because, as living goes on, and financial situations change, and desired economic destinations change, so will the use of your MAP change. But you will now have continual and immediate accountability and control over your finances. Your MAP will help get you from where you are to where you want to be.

Use the sample MAP on the following two pages to customize one for your notebook. Once you have refined it, type up one with the "actual" column blank and make 12 photocopies to use over the next year. Keep your Monthly MAP with your financial folder described earlier so that you will have easy access to everything you need for your monthly transactions.

III. SIMPLE SUGGESTIONS FOR SAVING

While you were applying your priorities to your expenses and adjusting them for cutbacks, the thought probably occurred to you, "Wait a minute; . . . just because I go through the list and reduce the amounts by certain percentages on a piece of paper doesn't necessarily mean that I can actually *spend less* every month. I need some guidance to help me know *how* to reduce my spending now that I have adjusted my MAP for the cutbacks."

Included in this section are over 225 ways for you to save money. Take the time to study the suggestions and determine whether or not you can assimilate them into your MAP. In the left margin by each bullet place an "A," "B," or "C" according to the following code:

A = I Do: I am presently taking advantage of this suggestion.

B = I Will: I will incorporate this suggestion into my MAP now.

C = Won't Work: There's no way this suggestion can be worked into my program.

At the end of each suggestion group *enter your score* and *decide on a plan* to incorporate the "I Wills" into your economic life-style.

MONTHLY MAP

Month of _____ Year _____

Expense Item	Projected Monthly Expense	Actual Monthly Expense
Tithe	_____	_____
Savings	_____	_____
Household:	_____	_____
Rent or mortgage payment	_____	_____
Gas, oil, wood	_____	_____
Electricity	_____	_____
Water	_____	_____
Telephone	_____	_____
Other: _____	_____	_____
Personal:	_____	_____
Food	_____	_____
Clothing	_____	_____
Dry cleaning	_____	_____
Hairdresser and barber	_____	_____
Allowances	_____	_____
Other: _____	_____	_____
Debts and Loans:	_____	_____
Automobile	_____	_____
College	_____	_____
Other: _____	_____	_____
Credit Cards _____	_____	_____
_____	_____	_____
_____	_____	_____
Transportation:	_____	_____
Car registration and license	_____	_____
Gas, diesel, oil	_____	_____
Commuting costs (tolls, bus, train, parking, etc.)	_____	_____
Insurance:	_____	_____
Automobile	_____	_____
Homeowners (not if included in house payment)	_____	_____

Expense Item	Projected Monthly Expense	Actual Monthly Expense
Health	_____	_____
Life	_____	_____
Medical:	_____	_____
Doctor (not covered by insurance)	_____	_____
Dental (not covered by insurance)	_____	_____
Drugs, prescriptions	_____	_____
Education:	_____	_____
Tuition, lessons	_____	_____
Educational supplies	_____	_____
Gifts:	_____	_____
Christmas	_____	_____
Weddings and anniversaries	_____	_____
Birthdays	_____	_____
Other: _____	_____	_____
Entertainment:	_____	_____
Eating out	_____	_____
Baby-sitting	_____	_____
Vacation	_____	_____
Sports and hobbies	_____	_____
Miscellaneous:	_____	_____
Child care	_____	_____
Child support, alimony	_____	_____
Other: _____	_____	_____
_____	_____	_____
TOTALS	$ _____	$ _____

Total Monthly Take-Home Pay $ _____
    (include any supplemental income this month)

Total Monthly Expenses $ _____

             BALANCE $ _____

A. Clothing

- Preplan your clothing purchases according to your MAP. Avoid impulse buying.
- Buy clothes in off-seasons.
- Buy certain items in quantity, i.e., four pairs of identical brown socks. When an individual sock wears or runs, you don't have to throw away the pair.
- Shop around, e.g., factory outlets, discount stores, stores that carry "seconds"; don't feel that you have to be loyal to one department store and buy all clothing there.
- Buy kids clothes with room for growth.
- Use good wood or plastic "shaped" hangers for your clothes. Hang them up immediately after getting out of them.
- Protect your investment in clothes, e.g., be prepared with a raincoat and boots.
- Keep hair spray and deodorants off your clothing.
- Change out of your good clothes before you cook or work if there is a possibility that you might get them damaged or dirty.
- Keep your clothes clean and mended; don't put off dry cleaning soiled clothes.
- Hang clothes in closets that have fresh air and are not humid or musty.
- Take advantage of using self-service, dry cleaning facilities.
- Pay attention to care instructions on the label.
- Choose traditional styles of clothing and shoes—add fashion accessories.
- Alternate pairs of shoes every day so the moisture can dry. (Two pairs of shoes worn alternately will outlast three pairs not alternated.)
- Wear shoes that fit, not just a certain size.
- Buy *quality material* and *workmanship*. (I would rather have a few nice, well-fitting clothes than a closet full of cheap fads.)
- If finances are tight, explore the possibility of buying clean used clothes from a thrift store.
- Try to trade for pressing, ironing, and dry cleaning.
- Remember, your clothes tell how you feel about yourself before you have a chance to speak. Decide what you want them to say, e.g.,
    "I want to blend into the crowd."
    "I see myself as a special person."

"I'm sloppy and really don't care."
"I'm very well organized."
"I'm faddish and up-to-date."
"I enjoy a creative touch."
"I'm plain, but I'm real quality."

- Make sure your clothes fit well. (Don't buy clothes a size small just because you think you will lose weight.)
- Purchase a basic garment and sew on your own "frills."
- Look at your clothes as an investment, i.e., choose them carefully, take care of them, expect a good return on your money.

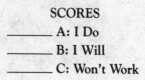

SCORES
_____ A: I Do
_____ B: I Will
_____ C: Won't Work

B. Medical/Health

- Do what your doctor tells you . . . exactly as he tells you. For example, if he says to lose 15 pounds, do it! If he says to take all the prescription, take it!
- Choose a doctor and have an appointment *before* you are sick.
- Even if you are well, have a checkup at least every three years.
- Choose your family doctor after asking questions and shopping around.
- Learn your normal weight and stick to it.
- Have your blood pressure checked regularly and keep it under control.
- Discuss fees with your doctor. You need not fear he will resent it.
- Save yourself and your regular doctor time by using the phone to discuss minor health problems. Talk to the nurse if possible.
- Ask your doctor about prescribing generic drugs. It's possible to save substantially. At least have him recommend an inexpensive pharmacy.
- If you require regular medication, you might want to explore the possibility of using reputable mail-order drug outlets. Ask your doctor about the following companies, and ask for a free catalog:

Getz Pharmacy
914 Walnut St.
Kansas City, MO 64106

Federal Prescription Service, Inc.
Second and Main St.
Madrid, IA 50156

Pastor's
126 S. York Rd.
Hatboro, PA 19040

- Ask your doctor for some free samples of your medication. He gets complimentary supplies.
- Make sure you are not paying a prescription price for a drug that is also available over the counter.
- Explore low-cost medical alternatives in your community. Immunizations or booster shots for entering school are many times done free at your local health department. Call your city health office to find out where you can get simple medical procedures, e.g., blood pressure, etc., performed free.
- When choosing a hospital, shop around—they don't all charge the same.
- Insist on an itemized cost breakdown, not just "medical expenses."
- See if your doctor is affiliated with a hospital that is a teaching institution or research center. Those hospitals have sources of revenue and talent not available to many hospitals.
- If at all possible, don't check into a hospital on Friday . . . check in on Tuesday.
- Consider a semiprivate room rather than insist on a private room.
- Explore the possibility of "PAT" . . .. *Pre-Admission Testing.* Check into the hospital for surgery but not for three days of tests that can be performed as an outpatient prior to the surgery.
- Explore the possibility of "walk-in surgery," i.e., in-and-out-the-same-day operation, including D & C, hernia, hemorrhoidectomy, biopsy, skin graft, vasectomy, etc.
- Many *unnecessary operations* are performed. Get a second opinion before you agree to an operation. The government is concerned enough about this situation that it maintains a toll-free hot line where you can find the name of another doctor in your area who is willing to act as a second consultant (1-800-638-6833).
- Shop around for a good dentist. Talk to him about fees before the work is done. Question any bill you suspect to be a mistake.
- On your first visit to a dentist, check if he inquires about your past medical history, e.g., diabetes, hemophilia, etc., any allergies you might have, the name and phone number of your regular physician,

whether or not you are presently on medication, and whether he stresses preventative as well as curative oral health.

SCORES

_____ A: I Do

_____ B: I Will

_____ C: Won't Work

C. Transportation

- Check with the National Highway Traffic Safety Administration for customer assistance with tire and accessory purchases, advice on safety measures, or to ask questions about safety defects or recalls. (1-800-424-9393)
- Take advantage of car pooling. If you still need to be convinced of the wisdom of car pooling, write for the free booklet, "Rideshare and Save—A Cost Comparison," The Federal Highway Administration, Office of Public Affairs, Room 4208, Nassif Building, Washington, D.C. 20590.
- Predetermine how much you can pay for a car *before* you go shopping.
- Buy the smallest car that will fit your needs.
- Consider gasoline mileage, but don't presume that the car that gets the best mileage is the most economical.
- Purchase discount gas. It is as good as big-name brands.
- Purchase only options that you really use. Agree on the necessary options *before* you get to the dealership.
- Shop around, not only for the car itself, but also for the best deals in financing, insurance, and trade-ins.
- Be aware of telltale signs of a high-pressure agency, i.e., being handed over to different salespeople and managers, being worn down by long waits, or having firm quotes increased for some "reason." Walk right out if your suspicions are aroused.
- Always consider selling your old car yourself rather than using it as a trade-in on a new model.
- Understand the warranty terms and check the reputation of the service department.
- *Resist* the pressure to purchase a new car every year—or even every three years. Maintain your car carefully and wisely hang on to it.
- Make sure you don't buy a car the first day you go shopping.

- Consider your bank or credit union before you finance a car through a dealership.
- Consider your regular insurance agent before you purchase an insurance package through a dealership.
- Perfect the art of driving smoothly and steadily. (When my boys were learning to drive, I told them to imagine a full glass of water on the hood; the challenge was to drive without spilling it.)
- Keep tires properly inflated.
- Consider purchasing radial tires.
- Approximately one minute of idling uses the same amount of gas as it takes to restart; so shut off your engine when you are not using it to move your car.
- Empty out unnecessary weight from your car's trunk.
- If buying a used car, hire a trusted mechanic to check it out.
- Think ahead and try to cut down on trips by combining errands.
- Keep your car tuned up and in good repair.
- Make sure your wheels are properly aligned.
- Turn corners slowly.
- Use your air conditioner only when necessary . . . it can cost as much as 2.5 mpg.
- Drive the car you can afford until you can afford to drive the car you want.
- Consider the possibility of getting rid of at least one of your cars.
- When flying, fly night coach and save at least 20 percent.
- Be sure to take advantage of airline promotions and special discounts.
- Make travel arrangements far enough in advance to qualify for discounts.

SCORES
_____ A: I Do
_____ B: I Will
_____ C: Won't Work

D. Home and Utilities

- Have a contractor check out the house before you buy.
- Buy rather than rent if possible.
- Have your furnace serviced annually. If you use a forced-air heating system, change or clean the filters every four to six weeks.

- Make a complete pictorial inventory and positively identify all your belongings *before* you have a loss from fire or theft.

- Secure appraisals on household items of value, e.g., rings, watches, gemstones, heirlooms, etc.

- Be sure your house is adequately insulated, i.e., attic, walls, and floors over open areas or garages. Instead of putting $2,000 in some stock and earning $150 a year taxable income, why not consider investing the same in insulation with a return of $200 a year on your utility bill—tax free?

- Wrap your water heater with special fiberglass kit—but don't cover vents.

- Periodically drain water heater tank to remove sediment that hampers efficiency.

- Repair equipment rather than replace.

- Metal heat ducts should be insulated; make sure there are no loose joints or seams.

- Insulate copper hot water pipes that run through unheated areas of the house.

- If you heat with electricity, look into using a "heat pump" system.

- Seal all window frames and sashes and install storm windows and doors if possible.

- Close the damper on your fireplace every time it is not in use. If damper does not close tightly, consider installing glass doors or cut a board to exactly fit the fireplace opening.

- Consider an automatic clock, set-back thermometer for your heating system.

- Make sure drapes, carpet, or furniture are not blocking heating outlets.

- Consider installing a water-flow restrictor on your shower head.

- Consider a solar unit to heat your water. (A $1,000 investment that saves you $200 per year gives you a 20 percent return on your money—tax free.)

- Repair all leaky faucets quickly.

- Keep the heat reflectors clean and shiny below the heating elements of your kitchen stove.

- Make sure your dishwasher is full, but not overloaded, when you turn it on.

- Open dishwasher after the rinse cycle so the dishes can air dry.

- Periodically vacuum dust from coils of refrigerator and freezer.

- Make sure the seals around your refrigerator doors and ovens are air tight.
- Take advantage of utility companies' energy audits under the Energy Act's Residential Energy Conservation Program. They will tell you how to save on fuel and energy costs.
- Use discretion when purchasing service contract on appliances. Be sure that it is not duplicating your warranty coverage.
- When shopping for refrigerators, freezers, dishwashers, water heaters, air conditioners, furnaces, etc., look for the yellow and black *Energy Guide* label which will tell you approximately how much the appliance will cost you to operate for one year.
- Consult the consumer buying guides before purchasing appliances.
- Take advantage of inexpensive firewood. Send for your copy of *Firewood for Your Fireplace, No. 559* from the Forest Service, U.S. Department of Agriculture, Washington, D.C. 20013.
- Read your utility bills and check meters for accuracy.
- Protect your furniture in high, dry climates (like Colorado) by installing a humidifier.
- Save on phone bills by dialing long distance direct in off hours.
- Remember to get credit for wrong numbers and cutoffs.
- Make sure phone bills are correct.
- Before you make a long-distance call to an establishment in another city, first check the *toll-free operator* to see if the number can be called at no cost to you. (1-800-555-1212)
- Set up a specific time for college kids to call home by *dialing direct*. It can save $500 over four years for two kids.
- Consider planting deciduous trees or vines on the west, south, and east sides of your house. The shade from the leaves will protect you from the summer sun, and when the leaves fall, the warm sunshine will be able to penetrate and help heat the house in winter.

SCORES
_____ A: I Do
_____ B: I Will
_____ C: Won't Work

E. Food and Shopping

- Avoid impulse buying . . . remember, impulse buying is your MAP's number-one enemy.

- With gasoline at today's prices, take into consideration the travel expense of running all over town for "bargains."

- Watch the prices of the items as they are being entered on the cash register at the check-out stand. You can often catch costly mistakes.

- Invest in a small, inexpensive calculator to carry with you while shopping.

- Use your calculator to quickly figure unit prices.

- Buy your staple items first and keep track of the total on your calculator . . . you will probably buy fewer "extras" if you know how much you've already spent.

- Preferably go grocery shopping only once a week.

- Shop when you are not hungry . . . there will be less temptation for impulse buying.

- Make sure that the nongrocery items purchased at the grocery store cannot be purchased less expensively elsewhere.

- Shop only from a prepared shopping list and discipline yourself to purchase only the items listed.

- With prices increasing so rapidly, it pays to look on all the different shelves in order to find items still marked at the old price.

- Try to avoid junk foods and snack foods; you can easily cut 10 to 15 percent from your grocery bill.

- Plan your menus around advertised and seasonal specials . . . especially meat specials.

- Consider buying turkey. It has a high ratio of meat to carcass, therefore is usually a very good buy . . . the bigger the bird, the more meat it will have in proportion to bone.

- Be creative in your slicing and preparing of meat. "A Dozen Ways to Stretch Your Beef Dollar" and "Money-saving Recipes" are two booklets you can receive by sending a stamped, self-addressed, business-size envelope to National Livestock and Meat Boards, Booklets, 444 N. Michigan Ave., Chicago, IL 60611.

- Check into the "no-frill" stores where you can pay up to 40 percent less for your groceries. You have to provide your own bags, do your own packing, and purchase from merchandise displayed in its original cartons.

- Buy ham and cheese ends. They are usually 50 percent of the regular price.

- Watch multiple pricing, e.g., 3 for $1.00 . . . they are not necessarily "specials."

- Make your own baby foods with the aid of a food blender.
- When you cook eggs alone, i.e., fried, poached, etc., use Grade A. When you use them in a recipe, use Grade B.
- Serve soup or salad as an appetizer . . . they will blunt the appetite. Then you won't have to serve as much main course.
- Get into the habit of reading the labels to determine the percentage of each ingredient. They will be listed in order of quantity, i.e., a can of stew that has peas listed first will probably have more peas than any other ingredient.
- Studies show that women buy fewer groceries on impulse than men or children. Ladies, leave the family at home and shop alone.
- Be aware of per serving pricing, e.g., if you send an apple in a lunch, it can be a small apple and do the same job as a huge apple.
- Really go easy on any prepared or convenience foods . . . you pay a lot for the convenience.
- Make your own TV dinners from leftovers.
- Get into the habit of using fortified dry milk for cooking.
- If you want to keep a very tight control on your shopping, record every grocery item purchased along with its price on a separate 3″ x 5″ card. Make your shopping list from your cards and calculate the cost while you are still home.
- Be wise when purchasing generic items versus brand-name items. Generic items are not necessarily bargains, e.g., plastic bags may be weaker and tear more easily and detergents may be only half strength, thus taking twice the amount for the same result, etc.
- Usually "house brands" are your best buy; just be sure you compare the weight and volume and not just the size of the container.
- You can usually save about 20 percent if you buy such items as flour and sugar in bulk bags rather than boxes.
- Purchase economy-size items only if you can use them up before they are wasted.
- Consider joining or organizing a food co-op. For information on food buying clubs, write: The Cooperative League of the U.S.A., Suite 1100, 1828 L St. N.W., Washington, D.C. 20036.
- It's still smart to grow and can your own food.
- Try playing the coupon-refund game. It takes some effort and organization to play. For information on how to play, write to American Coupon Club, Inc., P.O. Box 1149, Great Neck, NY 11023. Cost is $2.00.

SCORES

_____ A: I Do

_____ B: I Will

_____ C: Won't Work

F. Money/Credit

- Give careful consideration to all factors involved when borrowing money. There are occasions when it makes good sense to borrow, but realize that anytime you use O.P.M. (Other People's Money), you must pay for it.

- *Make certain* that the benefits for borrowing far exceed the cost of the loan liability.

- Borrow for a purchase only after you have had sufficient time to consider all factors involved. Never borrow for an impulse purchase.

- Always remember and make your decisions in light of the fact that you can never afford to purchase an ego trip with borrowed money.

- Make sure that what you purchase will last longer than it takes to pay for it; in fact, a good goal is to never purchase a depreciable item on credit.

- If you are borrowing to meet your current overhead, you're in trouble. Take the necessary steps to get your finances under control.

- If you purchase an item with an installment contract, be sure to *read* and *understand* all the provisions of the contract.

- Be sure all blanks of an installment contract are filled in.

- Work on being able to resist sales pressure.

- Make certain that credit purchases always have the spouse's approval; otherwise, there will never be the consistent discipline needed to meet the payments.

- *Co-sign only* if you are ready, willing, and able . . . and exceedingly happy to pay off the entire debt by yourself tomorrow without receiving any personal benefit whatsoever.

Unless you have the extra cash on hand, don't countersign a note. Why risk everything you own? They'll even take your bed! (Prov. 22:26, 27, TLB).

Son, if you endorse a note for someone you hardly know, guaranteeing his debt, you are in serious trouble. You may have trapped yourself by your agreement. Quick! Get out of it if you possible can! Swallow your pride; don't let embarrassment stand in the way. Go and beg to have your name erased. Don't put it off. Do it now. Don't rest until you do. If you can get out of this trap you have saved yourself like a deer that escapes from a hunter, or a bird from the net (Prov. 6:1-5, TLB).

- Your goal should be to use your credit card only if you can pay off the entire amount by the due date, before interest costs begin to be charged—sometimes at 21.6 percent.
- Control your credit card. If you cannot properly handle your credit card, then don't use it.
- Use discretion in borrowing and investing money. It doesn't make sense to borrow money at 11 percent and maintain a savings account at 5.25 percent.
- If you borrow, shop for the most inexpensive money you can find.
- Explore the possibility of borrowing low-interest educational loans that don't have to be paid back until the student is out of school.
- Explore the possibility of borrowing against a whole-life insurance policy at five to six percent.
- Consider removing cash from a bank that pays you little or no interest.
- Be sure you understand the terms of your NOW account (Negotiable Order of Withdrawal). You may not be getting what you think; all NOW accounts are *not* the same.
- Make sure your employer is not withholding more than he should from your check. The government will not pay you interest on excess withholdings.
- Consider fringe benefits rather than cash raises; they are not usually taxable.
- Consider placing savings into custodial accounts for your children. More than likely, they will not have to pay tax on the interest. Essentials for the children can be purchased from those accounts.
- Keep your credit record clean . . . it's important today . . . it will be more important tomorrow!
- Be honest in your credit applications, and pay your obligations on time.
- Consider nearly *anything* as a better alternative to bankruptcy.
- If you experience a legitimate payment problem, go immediately to the lender, explain the situation, and work out an agreeable arrangement. It's possible that you can even save your credit rating.
- The trend is more and more toward "electronic money." Make the effort to stay informed as to how that will affect you personally.

- Protect your credit cards as if they were cash, e.g., periodically check and make sure they are all in your possession.
- If a credit card is lost or stolen, know who to contact immediately to limit your liability.
- Make a promise to yourself—and keep it—that you will never loan out your credit card.
- Take care of your credit cards. Never leave your credit card in the glove compartment of your car or lying around in your office or hotel room.
- Be sure you have registered all your credit card numbers in your notebook for quick reference.
- TV advertising will more than likely disproportionately influence your purchasing habits. Shop around and discover bargains never mentioned on TV.
- Keep your priorities correct. If you can't afford to pay your tithe and set aside ten percent per month in savings, then you should not be borrowing.
- If you have diligently worked your way through this book, have conscientiously filled out your MAP, and have tried to follow it . . . and you are *still* head over heels in financial trouble, it is recommended that you seek help from some professional, Christian, financial counselor. If there is no Christian counseling available to you, consider contacting one of the Consumer Credit Counseling Services listed in your local Yellow Pages.

SCORES

_____ A: I Do

_____ B: I Will

_____ C: Won't Work

G. Insurance

AUTO:

- Shop around! Rates can vary from $200 to $300 for the same coverage.
- Make sure you have the type of coverage you think you have.
- Pay the highest "deductible" you can afford to pay—approximately one week's pay is a good rule of thumb, or approximately five percent of the car's value. That margin of "self insurance" can save you from 20 to 50 percent. I have observed that most people who are "fully insured" won't submit a claim for a small amount anyway,

because they are afraid if they turn it in, there will be an effect on the policy or the premium rate.

- Consider dropping collision and comprehensive coverage if your car is worth less than $1,000. You'll not collect more than the value of your car regardless of the cost to repair it.
- In today's economy make sure you have sufficient liability coverage. Judges are handing down big settlements.
- Check to see if you qualify for special discounts.

  ☐ Students with driver training
  ☐ Students with good scholastic average
  ☐ Cars with special safety features
  ☐ Over 25 and married
  ☐ No smoking or drinking
  ☐ Senior citizen with good record
  ☐ Low-mileage driver

- Eliminate duplicate coverage.
- If you have begun car pooling and have cut down on your driving, tell your insurance agent. Try to get a better rate.
- If you change jobs and end up working closer to home, contact your agent.
- If you are canceled for some reason, make sure you know why; make sure the company has all the facts correct.

HEALTH:

- Today's fancy computers will probably keep you from collecting twice for the same illness . . . so it probably won't pay you to carry duplicate coverage.
- Know your insurance coverage. Don't pay for coverage you don't need—e.g., maternity benefits when you are 90 (unless your names are Abraham and Sarah).
- Make sure your policy covers children from the *day of birth* and not from the age of two weeks.
- Stay away from paying interest on installment premiums.
- Take advantage of group policies. You almost always will get a better rate if you are included in a group policy.
- See if there is a provision for converting the group coverage to individual coverage in case you leave the group.
- Make sure you *understand* your coverage.
- If you have a $100 deductible on prescriptions, make sure you *collect* on any additional prescriptions.

- Make sure the doctor or hospital itemizes all charges; your insurance might not cover your exam, but it might cover the X-rays included in the exam.
- Check into "hospital indemnity insurance" which pays *in addition* to any other policy without risk of "duplication."
- Pay the highest "deductible" possible, but make sure you are well covered on major medical expenses.
- Keep your insurance agent apprised of any important family or health changes.

HOMEOWNERS:

- Consider coverage with a $500 deductible.
- Shop around for the best deal. Remember, all coverage is not the same, all prices are not the same.
- Insure your house for at least 80 percent of its replacement cost; change the amounts to keep up with inflation.
- Make adequate inventory of your contents—*now*, not *after* a loss.
- Beware of *overinsurance*. There is no need to overinsure your house.
- Consider a *tenant's policy* if you don't own the house.
- Check the possibility of qualifying for coverage offered through your professional organization, e.g., teacher's union, etc.
- Make sure you understand the limitations of your coverage. For unique or excessive household possessions, you may need a rider on your policy.

LIFE:

- Seriously shop around and compare before you buy. Many people purchase life insurance from a relative or friend just because of the pressure—be wise. Premiums can vary to 50 percent or more for equivalent coverage.
- Make sure that any life policy is based on *current* mortality tables.
- Try to buy any life insurance through a group plan; you can save up to 40 percent and medical exams are often waived.
- Know *what kind* of life insurance you are buying. Basically there are two types:

    1. *TERM:* the simplest, least costly type of coverage. It gives you coverage for a specific term . . . if you die, they pay.

    2. *WHOLE or ORDINARY or STRAIGHT:* a *savings plan* is added to your coverage known as "living benefits" or "cash values."

- In today's economy consider purchasing *term insurance* and *do your own* saving and investing. It won't be difficult to make more than the three to four percent offered with "whole" policies.
- Know and be aware that commissions are much higher on "whole" life policies than on "term."
- Consider renewable term protection which allows you to renew and continue coverage even if your health deteriorates.
- If you have been paying for a whole-life policy for many years, don't just drop it; see if it can be converted to some type of paid-up policy.
- Reevaluate your coverage regularly to make sure you have all you need—and no more. Invite two or three competing life insurance salesmen to present you with an analysis.
- Possibly reduce or drop certain coverage if your children have grown and are supporting themselves.
- Possibly reduce or drop certain coverage if your original beneficiary of your policy has died or become financially independent.
- Possibly reduce or drop certain coverage if your have savings or liquid investments that would cover death costs, taxes, and emergency needs.
- Possibly reduce or drop certain coverage as you become debt free.
- Periodically, reevaluate your need for insurance. Don't be surprised if you discover that you don't need to keep paying for life insurance coverage for the same reasons you once did.
- Avoid insurance by mail schemes.
- Investigate the newest types of "health awareness" or "physical fitness" policies.

SCORES
_____ **A: I Do**
_____ **B: I Will**
_____ **C: Won't Work**

H. Merchandise

There is currently a great amount being written explaining the virtues of *investing in merchandise* as a valid hedge against inflation. It has its premise in a principle which we discussed earlier: i.e., *because of the present economic and tax structure, it is often more profitable to save tax-free dollars than it is to earn dollars that are subject to exorbitant taxation.* Remember: a penny saved can be *more* than a penny earned.

Wisely investing in merchandise which you know you will use in the future can return to you a higher tax-free dividend, in many cases, than putting your money out at a nominal interest amount which is subject to reduction by taxation.

For example, Christmas cards can be purchased at post-season sales with savings of at least 50 percent. You know that next year you will buy Christmas cards, and you also know that next year you will pay *more* for the very same cards. If you can purchase a box of cards regularly priced this year at $25.00 but marked down to $12.50, you will have made a significant savings. But, because of inflation, next year the same box of cards will sell for $27.50. Your $12.50 investment will have given you a 120 percent return on your money—a yield that is tough to beat—and it's tax free.

Bargain sales of cleaning supplies, canned goods, health and beauty products, staple foods, paper and plastic products, traditional clothing, home and yard equipment, towels, sheets, etc., are obvious candidates for merchandise investing. In fact, anything that is not perishable, not too bulky to store, and not likely to go out of style might be considered. Items that could be used to *trade* might be considered as well as items you would use personally.

The concept is simple: If you know your money is going to devaluate and you know prices are going to increase, then *convert your money to items that will enable you to preserve your original purchasing power.* As you will recall from Chapter Four, not only do prices increase with inflation, but the increased number of earned dollars that you are required to use to pay for the increased prices puts you into a higher tax bracket. Therefore, you are penalized on both ends of the deal, i.e., the "double whammy." Converting your money to merchandise can preserve your purchasing power.

One caution, however, is to not use your stocked merchandise at a faster rate than you would have if you had to pay as you used it. For instance, if you have a dozen new bath towels stored in the attic, don't discard your still usable ones just because they've faded slightly.

I hope that, as you have gone through this chapter on saving all you can, you have more clearly realized the importance of old-fashioned frugality.

8

Give All You Can

INTRODUCTION

Your giving is expected to come out of that which has been deposited into your personal Trust Account. In Chapters Six and Seven you were asked to explore the ideas of *earn all you can* and *save all you can* so that you will be in a better position to *give all you can*. Remember that as you give all you can, God has a chance to bless those gifts and multiply them and return them to your Trust Account . . . in the form of compensating balances *so that* you can give them out again.

The *motivation* behind your accumulation should be the recognized opportunities for distribution. The Bible says:

> Give, and it will be given to you. A good measure, pressed down, shaken together and running over, will be poured into your lap (Lk. 6:38a, NIV).
>
> Whatever measure you use to give—large or small—will be used to measure what is given back to you (Lk. 6:38b, TLB).

An old proverb says:

> What I hoard I lose.
> What I try to keep will be left and fought over by others.
> What I give will continue to return . . . forever.

In this chapter the subject of "give all you can" will be reviewed from three vantage points:
  I. Give while you are still alive
 II. Give after you are gone
III. Creative methods of giving

153

I. GIVE WHILE YOU ARE STILL ALIVE

A. The Positive Privilege of Tithing

Throughout my life I have observed that some people struggle with the concept of tithing. *Tithe* means one tenth. *Tithing* is devoting the *first tenth* of your income to God and His Kingdom. Usually, the only reason people ever have a struggle over tithing is simply because they do not completely understand the concept.

You do not tithe just because it's written in the Law that you must tithe, even though that isn't a bad reason. But tithing the firstfruits of your income has always been part of God's economic plan—long before the Law was ever handed down to Moses. Melchizedek, the King of Salem, was also a priest of the most high God (Genesis 14 and Hebrews 7). Abraham paid tithe to that high priest in approximately 1883 B.C.—over 425 years *before* the Law was ever given to Moses. That 4,000-year-old example is to be followed by us today as we give our gifts to Christ, of whom the Scriptures declare: "You are a priest forever with the rank of Melchizedek" (Heb. 7:17b, TLB).

Jacob, when confronted by God in his "ladder-day" experience at Bethel, vowed two things to God: (1) I will choose Jehovah as my God! (2) I will give you back a tenth of everything you give me! (cf., Gen. 28:21b, 22b).

When it became necessary for the Law to be written down, God certainly never overlooked the beautiful concept of tithing.

> You must tithe all of your crops every year . . . this applies to your tithes of grain, new wine, olive oil, and the firstborn of your flocks and herds. *The purpose of tithing is to teach you always to put God first in your lives* (Deut. 14:22, 23, TLB, emphasis added).

Every place God commanded tithing He balanced it by promising that *if you put Him first, He would see to it that your needs would be met by His sufficiency!* Solomon attested to that principle nearly 500 years after the Law was written.

> Honor the Lord by giving him the first part of all your income, and he will fill your barns with wheat and barley and overflow your wine vats with the finest wines (Prov. 3:9, 10, TLB).
>
> In everything you do, put God first, and he will direct you and crown your efforts with success (Prov. 3:6, TLB).

Less than 400 years before Christ was born, the Hebrew people had forgotten God's commands. To put it quite plainly, they had made an absolute mess out of their lives and their nation. They had changed.

But the prophet Malachi appeared to remind them that God doesn't change: before the Law, in the Law, or after the Law.

> "For I am the Lord—I do not change . . . Though you have scorned my laws from earliest time, *yet you may still return to me* . . . Come and I will forgive you.
> "But you say, 'We have never even gone away!'
> "Will a man rob God? Surely not! And yet you have robbed me.
> " 'What do you mean? When did we ever rob you?'
> "You have robbed me of the tithes and offerings due to me. And so the awesome curse of God is cursing you, for your whole nation has been robbing me. *Bring all the tithes into the storehouse so that there will be food enough in my Temple; if you do, I will open up the windows of heaven for you and pour out a blessing so great you won't have room enough to take it in!*
> *"Try it! Let me prove it to you!* Your crops will be large, for I will guard them from insects and plagues. Your grapes won't shrivel away before they ripen," says the Lord of Hosts. "And all nations will call you blessed, for you will be a land sparkling with happiness. These are the promises of the Lord of Hosts" (Mal. 3:6-12, TLB, emphasis added).

Then came Christ! His personal claims were that He came not to destroy any of the Law, but to fulfill it. He declared that "Yes, you should tithe." It is a good place to start . . . *but a tragic place to quit.*

> Yes, woe upon you, Pharisees, and you other religious leaders—hypocrites! For you tithe down to the last mint leaf in your garden, but ignore the important things—justice and mercy and faith. *Yes, you should tithe, but you shouldn't leave the more important things undone* (Mt. 23:23, TLB, emphasis added).

While proclaiming nothing that would in any way weaken the position of the Law on tithing, Christ went on to teach *a more excellent way,* a way of making available to God 100 percent of everything in your Personal Portfolio of Possessions in an attitude and act of complete commitment.

> As he stood in the Temple, he was watching the rich tossing their gifts into the collection box. Then a poor widow came by and dropped in two small copper coins.
> "Really," he remarked, "this poor widow has given more than all the rest of them combined. For they have given a little of what they didn't need, but she, poor as she is, *has given everything she has"* (Lk. 21:1-4, TLB, emphasis added).

Christ knew that "Tithing . . . plus . . ." must become a way of life. He taught that the failure to give all is simply a failure to understand God's character . . . *but in giving all, the very character of God is developed in the giver.*

Anyone who takes care of a little child like this is caring for me! And whoever cares for me is caring for God who sent me. *Your care for others is the measure of your greatness* (Lk. 9:48, TLB, emphasis added).

Today, tithing is simply your testimony to God's total ownership. It is an *external evidence* of an *internal commitment*, an *outward expression* of an *inward attitude*. I am *thankful* for the size of my tithe check—I have been blessed into that position. Tithing is not a heavenly insurance policy against hassle or persecution; but I have found that tithe, when given as a testimony, always reaps great dividends because God is then able to take direct control over that which He owns anyway and multiply it accordingly. And somehow I always have a sufficient amount left over—plus the imparted wisdom to manage it wisely. I'm certain that being faithful in my tithing has done far more for me than my mere money has done for the Kingdom!

> It is possible to give away and become richer! It is also possible to hold on too tightly and lose everything. Yes, the liberal man shall be rich! By watering others, he waters himself (Prov. 11:24, 25, TLB).

The *purpose* then of tithing, as you learned from Deuteronomy 14, *"is to teach you always to put God first in your lives."* It is a privilege to be able to tithe—a method of giving while you are still alive.

B. Additional Giving Beyond the Tithe

Another method of giving while you are still living is through the sharing of *offerings*. Offerings are those possessions beyond your tithe which are transferred from *your* Trust Account into the Trust Account of *others* (TAT). But how will you know *when* or *how much* you should give to others?

Many times your offerings will be given through your organized church, and they will corporately determine worthwhile projects. But other times you will be called on to make a TAT on a personal basis. A good rule of thumb to follow is: *never keep what the Holy Spirit says to give*. Offerings, of course, would include the giving of money, but should also include anything transferred from your Personal Portfolio of Possessions, e.g., talents, friendship, concern, etc.

More than likely, your greatest fulfillment in living will be realized through your giving. Start looking for ways to live more fully by finding ways to give more completely. You will find a positive correlation between your giving behavior and your spiritual strength.

C. Diversified Motivations for Giving

The *motive* that prompts the gift is worthy of examination. God wants your gifts to come from a heart of cheerful, complete commitment. "Don't force anyone to give more than he really wants to, for cheerful givers are the ones God prizes" (II Cor. 9:6, TLB).

It is said that the final temptation is the greatest treason: to do the right thing . . . for just the wrong reason. And I am sure that you have observed gifts being given from less than ideal motives. Look now at some of those motives.

1. Occasionally the situation may force a person into giving . . . e.g., social pressure, etc. The problem is that it wasn't so much a gift as it was a method of buying one's way out of the pressure. *Can you think of a time when that happened to you or someone you know? Describe the situation in your notebook.*

2. Occasionally someone gives just to be seen and receive an ego stroke. Usually the giver will take great pains to see that the gift is well recorded. *Can you think of a time when that happened to you or someone you know? Describe the situation and how it turned out in your notebook. Can you recall a Scripture where this type of giving is mentioned?*

3. Sometimes a gift is given simply because the cause needs it and deserves it. The cause has good appeal, and there is almost a guilt trip if there is not a response to the appeal. *Can you think of a time when that happened to you or someone you know? Describe it in your notebook.*

4. Other giving is motivated by an overflowing heart of love and thanksgiving . . . where there is no limitation of expectancy at all . . . just willing relinquishment. *Relate some examples of that motivation working out through your life or as you have observed it in the lives of others.*

> Tell them to use their money to do good. They should be rich in good works and should give happily to those in need, always being ready to share with others whatever God has given them (I Tim. 6:18, TLB).

II. GIVE AFTER YOU ARE GONE

A. Your Final Act of Stewardship

Much of your giving will be accomplished while you are still alive. But you also have the *opportunity* of giving after you are gone. Upon your death you have the responsibility of properly disposing of all the residual possessions in your Trust Account. Even at death, you are responsible to God for *everything* He has allowed you to possess during life. Your Last Will and Testament will possibly become your *grandest testimony of stewardship.*

B. Extended Giving Through a Will

What is a will? According to *Black's Law Dictionary,* a will is: "A written instrument executed with the formalities of law, whereby a person makes a disposition of his property to take effect after his death." Your will is a written testimony of your desires regarding the distribution of what is left over in your Personal Possession Portfolio after you are gone. The will is supported by legal powers which you delegate to individuals or to institutions to carry out your desires. The execution of your desires is enforced by the probate court.

No doubt you have heard the phrase *"Last Will and Testament."* A *testator* is a person who has a will. If a person with a will dies, he is said to have died *"testate."* If a person dies without having a will, he is said to have died *"intestate."*

It has been said that your will is the most important document of your life next to your birth certificate and your marriage license. But, surprisingly, not everyone knows that. It is estimated that *seven out of ten people in the United States die without leaving a will!*

When you die intestate (without a will), you *forfeit* your right to dispose of your possessions and guardianship responsibilities according to your own desires. Your estate will be divided and administered according to the intestacy laws of the state in which you live.

- Wouldn't you like to have some say in choosing the personal representative of your estate?
  Without a will, the personal representative is named according to the laws of the state.

- If you died, survived by minor children and no spouse, wouldn't you like to have some say about the children's new guardians?
  Without a will, guardianship is determined by the state.

- As a sole proprietor of a business, wouldn't you like to give guidance as to the continuation or liquidation of that business?
  Without a will, you cannot leave specific instructions.

- Wouldn't you like to help decide how your estate is divided?
  Without a will, your estate will be divided according to state law.

- Wouldn't you like to be a part of deciding which church, hospital, college, missionary outreach, local charity, or needy friend would receive a portion of those assets remaining in *your* Personal Possession Portfolio?
  Without a will, there can be no gifts or charities of any kind directed after your death to specific recipients.

- If you die with no survivors, wouldn't you like to have something to say as to the distribution of any or all of your estate?
  Without a will and no surviving relatives close enough in kinship to inherit . . . the state will take it all.

One way to look at it is, the state has already written a will for you. It has promised to distribute your possessions *without your expressed consent* upon your death. The only way to alter that plan of distribution is for you to counter it with an expressed will of your own. Faithful stewardship must include a plan for final distribution.

C. Seek the Help of the Professionals

If you do not have a will, you need the help of a qualified lawyer. The state laws require certain legal formalities in the execution of a will. If certain formalities are ignored, even the simplest will may be invalid.

The tax consequences of dying without a *valid* will are tremendous. But with a proper will and sound tax counsel, you will be able to preserve significant amounts of money or your assets from the tax collector and direct them to the areas of your choice.

Existing wills should be reviewed periodically by legal counsel. For those of you who have had wills drawn and estate planning incorporated into those wills prior to 1986, you will need to have them reviewed as soon as possible. The Economic Recovery Tax Act of 1986 has made much traditional estate planning obsolete.

If your will was executed while you were living in another state, you should have it reviewed to make sure it complies with the laws of the state in which you presently reside.

Often people ask if they can change their will if certain situations should change in their family, finances, or occupations. The answer is "yes, you can change your will." But you cannot make the changes just by altering the face of your present will. Such alterations may invalidate your will. It takes either a new will to replace the old one or formal codicils to effectively alter the old.

Should a wife have a will? Yes! for at least two reasons. *First*, even if she does not presently have ownership of any property in her name, she no doubt will inherit a portion of her husband's estate at his death and should have a will for the disposition of that property. *Second*, a wife should have a will, drawn so it doesn't conflict with the provisions of her husband's, in the event that both should die simultaneously. That will predetermine the answers to questions of guardianship and trusteeship. Attorneys usually charge only a nominal amount for drafting the will for the spouse.

A single parent should never be without a valid will.

It usually is wisest to keep your will in a safe place, but where it can be readily located. Some attorneys will, upon request, keep the original will in their file. Some states permit wills to be deposited with the probate court, prior to death, for safekeeping. Don't leave it where it will be stolen, forgotten, or lost. If you would like, you can keep a copy of the will in your home and inform someone of its location and the location of the original will. It is usually not a part of wisdom to keep the original in your own safe-deposit box, since the box will be sealed in some states by the tax officials upon your death. A sealed safe-deposit box can cause a great amount of frustration for a family already in bereavement. Your spouse, or the individual you've named as personal representative, should be apprised of where you keep your will.

D. Supply Your Attorney with Needed Information

Certainly, your will should reflect your own personal wishes and desires. But there is no way your attorney can guess what those wishes and desires might be . . . unless you communicate to him exactly how you feel about your estate. You must be complete in the disclosure of your possessions and open in your desires for distribution. It is very important to seek counsel from a *Christian attorney* who will understand your set of values and respect your commitment to God.

In order to conserve your attorney's time—and save you money—there are some areas of information that you can compile and organize that will be helpful in writing your will. It is suggested that you gather the information, write it down, and have it ready before you go in for your appointment. The information will not only help your attorney draw your will, but will also aid the administration of your estate.

If you have been faithfully filling out your notebook, you will already have much of the information at your fingertips. Your list should include:

- Names, addresses, birth dates, and birthplaces of yourself, your spouse, children, parents, brothers, and sisters. Indicate if any are incompetent or handicapped.
- If you have more than one residence, you should specify how much time you spend at each, where you pay your income taxes, and where you vote.
- List the Social Security numbers of you and your spouse, and specify where cards are located.
- List names of previous spouses either deceased or divorced.
- Indicate the location of your marriage license, birth certificate, veteran's discharge papers, divorce or separation papers (if previously married), and copies of previous tax returns.
- List your accountant's name and any additional attorneys who might have any of your important papers in their possession.

- List names and addresses of all persons, organizations, or institutions you plan to make beneficiaries. Make certain the names are legally correct.
- Name any agreements where *you* are the beneficiary, trustee, personal representative, or guardian.
- Give as complete as possible details on desired funeral arrangements. Preplanning can save from 50 to 75 percent of the ordinary costs presented to your family at the time of death. (Don't let a mortician get the chance to make your family feel guilty or disrespectful for economizing . . . write for a copy of *A Manual of Death Education and Simple Burial*, by Ernest Morgan, Celo Press, Burnsville, NC 28714; cost is $2.00 plus postage.)
- List all insurance or annuity policies:
  1. owned by you on your life,
  2. owned by others on your life,
  3. owned by you on others' lives.
  Indicate the name and address of each company, the name and address of agents, policy numbers, amounts, beneficiaries, loans on polices (if any), and who pays the premiums on each.
- List any benefits that would come to you from organizations to which you belong, e.g., unions, fraternal or trade groups, military service, etc.
- List your employer and specify any receivable benefits, e.g., stock purchase agreements, death benefits, bonuses due, profit-sharing plans, etc.
- List the location of any safe-deposit boxes and the location of the keys.
- Itemize your debts: real estate mortgages, personal loans, installment contracts, stock loans, etc.
- List any debts that have "credit life" insurance policies on them.
- Itemize your assets:
  1. Real estate—all properties owned, ownership status, location, current value, cost basis, mortgages, location of deeds, title policies.
  2. Other assets—stocks, stock options, bonds, money market certificates, securities (include name of stock firms and broker), loans or accounts receivable, bank accounts, ownership interests in businesses or partnerships, and rare or valuable personal property.
- Give names and addresses of persons you wish to act as guardians of your children, personal representative, and trustees of your estate.
- Should you be inclined to donate an organ (heart, eye, etc.), that

should be expressed by a document that you can carry on your person, so that it can be utilized immediately in the event of a fatal accident. Organ transplants must be done without the lapse of time. A lapse would occur if you had to wait until your will was located and read. Organ donation cards are readily available. Contact your medical doctor if you want to make such a TAT.

Even though you may have your "Last Will and Testament" drawn many years before you die, your will is your last expression of stewardship. It will stand as an ultimate testimony of your *recognition of God's ownership* and *your Agency Agreement with Him.*

III. CREATIVE METHODS OF GIVING

Fulfilling the admonition to give all you can can be very exciting. For instance, if you can multiply your gift by making it *tax deductible*, then see to it that it's tax deductible. If you can *creatively give something away now* and enjoy the satisfaction of seeing it being used for Kingdom business, then give it away now. If you can arrange for your employer to join you in a gift, *then don't hesitate to pursue the possibility.*

Here are a few suggestions for creatively multiplying your giving.

A. Tax-deductible Gifts

It is a recognized fact that the government cannot, through its benevolent programs, meet all the humanitarian needs of society. It may try . . . but it cannot! Therefore, the government has, through the years, depended upon the charitable giving of the private sector to make up the difference. For that supplemental charity, the government has been willing to allow favorable tax treatment for the contributors. Congress has encouraged private philanthropy for about the last 60 years through such favored tax treatment. When the gifts are given to a *qualified recipient,* tax deduction is granted. While the donor is alive, the amount of the deductible gift is subtracted from the adjusted gross income. Gifts given by a decedent are deductible from unified estate taxes.

When the government allows deductions for qualified charitable giving, it in essence is joining you in your gift. You give part of the gift . . . the government gives the rest. Have you ever thought of it that way? You actually obligate the government to give to the qualified charity of your choice. For example, if you decided to give $1,000 to your favorite qualified charitable organization, that $1,000 would be subtracted from your taxable income. If you are in the 50 percent tax bracket, it is possible that you just might salvage approximately $500. The net result of a tax-deductible gift is that you have *more left over to give.* You multiply your giving.

If you are counting on taking a tax deduction for a gift, you will first need to find out if the *recipient is qualified.* A charitable gift is tax deductible only if it is made to or for the use of a charitable organization qualified to receive such gifts. However, you should *never* withhold your hand in charity just because there's no way for the gift to qualify as a tax deduction. True Christian love cannot depend on the government's approval or participation.

Why is all this information important? Not all "nonprofit corporations" or "tax-exempt organizations" qualify to receive tax-deductible gifts. Anyone can file a "not-for-profit" corporation in their state. But that does not make the organization a qualified recipient. Many fine organizations, e.g., chambers of commerce, civic groups, fraternal societies, etc., are exempt from paying taxes . . . but do not necessarily qualify for receiving deductible contributions.

The Internal Revenue Service is the only entity that can approve an organization to receive deductible contributions, based on that organization's application. Most churches, schools, and hospitals have received their qualification status. The IRS periodically publishes a list of approved organizations . . . Treasury Publication 78, U.S. Government Printing Office, *Cumulative List of Organizations Described in Section 170(c) of the Internal Revenue Code of 1954.* If you are in question about an organization's deductible qualifications, phone the IRS, and they will tell you if it qualifies.

B. Methods of Deferred Giving

If you could receive an immediate tax deduction for a transfer of property that would not be consummated until some date in the future, i.e., your death or someone else's death, and you could retain the right to enjoy the property until that future date, would you be interested? Many people are interested. In fact, many people choose deferred giving as a way of making charitable contributions.

Deferred giving is not limited to real estate where you would, for example, give a piece of property to a church or college with the right to retain the property's benefits until you die. Deferred giving can even be applied to such things as corporate bonds where you would give the bonds and retain the right to the interest for an extended period of years. In many cases, deferred giving is like having your cake and eating it, too. But, in order to take advantage of deferred giving, you must utilize a qualified vehicle, such as:
- a charitable remainder annuity trust,

- a charitable remainder unitrust,
- a pooled income fund.

Your attorney or estate planner will be able to advise you which vehicle would be best if you wish to participate in a deferred gift.

C. Other Forms of Creative Giving

1. LIFE INSURANCE

It is possible to make an *outright contribution* of all rights of ownership in a life insurance policy and create an immediate deduction for income tax purposes. However, just naming a charitable organization as a beneficiary will not give you an immediate tax deduction. Some very creative giving can be done with life insurance policies, e.g., endowments, etc.

2. STOCK

Gifts of stock can be given to a charitable organization. If the organization would rather have cash at a later date, it can sell the stock. If it is a qualified recipient, it can even take advantage of the stock appreciation without tax consequence. Or, in the event of a corporate liquidation, a stockholder may want to contribute some of his stock to avoid a heavily taxable income position.

3. ART OBJECTS

There is usually no problem with your *giving* of art objects . . . usually the problem comes with how much IRS will allow you to count as a deduction. You will be expected to furnish detailed information to substantiate your deduction claim if the object is valued in excess of $200. The information should be in the form of an appraisal and should include the following:

a. *A listing of the appraiser's qualifications,*
b. *The appraiser's statement of value,*
c. *Information affecting the appraisal, e.g., any restrictions or limits to the use or disposition of the property,*
d. *The date of the appraisal,*
e. *The signature of the appraiser.*

The IRS is cracking down in some areas like this type of giving because of abuse. The IRS has allowed a contribution for the base amount of the property given, and not full fair-market value when there appears to be abuse or some scheme. In the event there is a considerable difference between your base amount and fair market value, the IRS may challenge you. Therefore, you will need to be able to prove your base amount, the length of time you have owned the property, and the circumstances which may have caused the object to appreciate so drastically or rapidly. You should be able to prove that you have held the object for not less than one year and a day. Holding the object just a little bit longer may benefit you considerably. In the event of any questions, consult your attorney or CPA for the present IRS rulings.

4. EMPLOYER/EMPLOYEE PARTICIPATION GIFTS

Recently, many corporations have been allowing their employees to suggest qualified charities of their choice to become beneficiaries of the corporation's giving. *What a great idea!* The corporation would otherwise lose that money through tax. But the participation program allows both the employer and employee to join together in the experience of giving. The company's check is made out to the qualified charity, given to the employee, who in turn gives it to the selected organization. The corporation gets the charitable contribution deduction, and the employee receives the satisfaction of being instrumental in the directed gift—without realizing any taxable income.

Be generous with what God has given to you. Remember, "Purity is best demonstrated by generosity" (Lk. 11:41, TLB). Accept the challenge to become the most *trustworthy administrator* possible of your *earthly trust account.*

EARN ALL YOU CAN
SAVE ALL YOU CAN
so that you can
GIVE ALL YOU CAN

When you think about it . . . the untrustworthy administrator really doesn't have much to which he or she can look forward. Jesus said that "if you are untrustworthy about worldly wealth, who will trust you with the true riches of heaven?" (Lk. 16:11, TLB). But for the *trustworthy* . . . what a different story! After you have lived out a beautiful life of giving and sharing, you have the indescribable opportunity of joyfully looking forward to God entrusting His true riches of eternity into your heavenly trust account when He declares:

"Well done, thou good and faithful servant: thou hast been *faithful over a few things, I will make thee ruler over many things:* enter thou into the joy of thy lord" (Mt. 25:21, KJV, emphasis added).

So, "What'cha gonna do with what'cha got?"

Phil 4:19